Praise

SPARK LEARNING

"*Spark Learning* by Ramsey Musallam explores the need to unlock student potential through creativity in a unique and thoughtful exploration. The book highlights ideas and advice that can help revolutionize your classroom."

—**ADAM BELLOW**, co-founder, Breakout EDU

"Through years of thoughtful reflection, Ramsey has developed a profound understanding of teaching and learning. This book gives the rest of the world a chance to walk the halls of his mind."

—**AARON SAMS**, author, EdTech leader, education faculty, St. Vincent College

"Ramsey presents a humble, relatable, and inspiring framework in *Spark Learning*, balanced with practical steps any educator can take. This is a call to action for educators everywhere to recognize their own influence and ability to embrace and encourage curiosity. All teacher education programs should have this as required reading!"

—**ELIZABETH BRUMBAUGH**, director of learning, innovation and design PreK–12, Harker School, San Jose, California

"I haven't encountered a more curious human than Ramsey Musallam. He's contagious in his ability to encourage inquiry, embrace the mess, and spark learning. I've been challenged to view my classroom and my job as an educator in an entirely new way that honors students at their very best—through the questions they ask."

—**MOLLY BENNETT**, executive director of Summits, EdTechTeam

"Ramsey has been one of my significant influencers in shaping my pedagogy. Get past 'pseudoteaching' and get students really curious about learning—not just gathering enough points to pass."

—ALICE KEELER, teacher,
author *50 Things You Can Do With Google Classroom*

"Ramsey captures the essence of what it means to pursue excellence in our teaching practice since our students and our communities deserve our best. Although we're not all surgeons doing lifesaving work every day, this analogy reminds us of the critical contributions that teachers can and do make daily. Thanks, Ramsey!"

—GREGORY T. RUSHTON, PhD, associate professor of chemistry,
Stony Brook University

"In a time when changes in education can seem inevitable and daunting, Ramsey and his book, *Spark Learning*, provide for us three concrete considerations that focus on the one constant—the child. A research-based examination of what inspires children to learn, *Spark Learning* is so humane that every teacher should read and experience its message."

—SEAN BEAVERSON, education technology specialist

"In *Spark Learning*, Ramsey Musallam offers us clear, concise instructions on how to harness the curiosity of students to fuel exploration and deepen learning. Musallam's own contagious enthusiasm, energy, and curiosity shine through in his writing, making *Spark Learning* an inspiring guide for any educator looking to up their game."

—SAMANTHA GRANT WIESLER, founder, GUSH Productions,
lecturer, UC Berkeley Graduate School of Journalism

"Ramsey Musallam pairs insightful research and enduring enthusiasm with practical examples that will resonate with all educators. His pursuit of the most impactful teaching practices, infectious optimism, and groundbreaking insights into student engagement and achievement make this book a must-read!"

—MARK GARRISON, director of technology and innovation

"Ramsey Musallam's affinity for curiosity is contagious, inspiring teachers all over the globe to bring curiosity to the forefront of learning. *Spark Learning* will do two things: provide you research-based, practical classroom applications and ignite a spark of curiosity in students!"

—LISA HIGHFILL, teacher, coach, author

"Dr. Musallam's insights into the experience of student learning and educator formation are valuable resources for teachers and administrators alike. His themes of curiosity, flexibility, and reflection resonate across all educational settings and inspire me to be my best as a teacher and leader."

—MIKE DANIELS, EdD, director, Office of Education,
Lasallian District of San Francisco New Orleans

"*Spark Learning* represents an opportunity for educators of all grade levels and content areas to 'reboot' their teaching style from a teacher who excels at reinventing learning for his students and inspires creativity among his fellow educators. Ramsey Musallam takes you through the three keys to embracing the power of student curiosity in this important pedagogical work for the twenty-first century."

—MIKE LAWRENCE, CEO, CUE

"*Spark Learning* translates the theory of creativity into practical steps to help any teacher jumpstart a 'curiosity-first curriculum' that has students begging for more."

—CHRIS FITZGERALD WALSH, education innovator and
entrepreneur

"Our world is advancing at an exponential rate; we need our youth to grow, think, and create beyond the traditional framework of our education system. Ramsey's *Spark Learning* is a must-read for anyone who believes we need to raise the next generation of problem solvers."

—CHRIS FORNELL SCOTT, educator, author, sailor

"I've read what Ramsey writes, and I've seen him speak, and he never fails to spark new ideas and curiosity in me. You'll find his thoughts intriguing, the examples practical, and the ten bonus strategies wonderful tools for making great things happen in your classroom!"

—RUSHTON HURLEY, founder, NextVista.org

"Dr. Musallam shares the formula of how to tap into the five senses that students are innately born with (but are often muted in the traditional classroom) in order to reach their full learning potential. I've seen this formula work firsthand and nobody demonstrates/lives the teachings better than Ramsey."

—DARREN HUDGINS, director of instructional technology, OETC

SPARK
LEARNING

3 Keys to Embracing the Power of Student Curiosity

RAMSEY MUSALLAM, EdD

Spark Learning
© 2017 by Ramsey Musallam

This book is available at special discounts when purchased in quantity for use as premiums, promotions, fundraisers, or for educational use. For inquiries and details, contact the publisher at books@daveburgessconsulting.com.

Published by Dave Burgess Consulting, Inc.
San Diego, CA
http://daveburgessconsulting.com

Cover Design by Genesis Kohler
Editing and Interior Design by My Writers' Connection

Library of Congress Control Number: 2017940077
Paperback ISBN: 978-1-946444-13-4
Ebook ISBN: 978-1-946444-14-1

First Printing: June 2017

BASED ON
RAMSEY MUSALLAM'S
POPULAR TED Talk
"3 RULES TO SPARK LEARNING"

bit.ly/3Rules2Spark

For additional ideas and resources visit
CyclesofLearning.com

To my present and past colleagues:
Through sharing (and stealing) ideas, late
night discussions, tense arguments, and
lots of messy learning, I wake up each day
energized to teach.

Thank you.

CONTENTS

FOREWORD

by Zander Nosler, founder and CEO of Kitsbow

Hopefully over the course of your own education, you encountered a teacher who was so compelling, so good, that they showed you what you were capable of doing, in an area well outside of your comfort zone. For me, it was my eleventh grade English teacher, Mrs. Weaver. Being more of a nerdy engineer type, I never made English—much less any of the humanities—my strong suit. But the culminating project for that class, a detailed literary analysis of a work of fiction of your choice, ended up being the crowning achievement of my high school career. The assignment at first was so daunting, I was resigned to struggle and fail. My memory of the project, however, was anything but failure. It started with the book *All the King's Men*—not exactly on the teenage top ten reading list, even back in the '80s. I remember reading it and asking Mrs. Weaver, "What's all the fuss about?" She asked me, "Well, what do you think this book is really about?" It was that question that got me thinking, *Wait. There's more here than I thought?* From that point forward we peeled back layers of meaning, and I pulled together a fifteen-page thesis of which I was actually proud.

Thinking back about Mrs. Weaver, I realize that what made her so effective was her ability to get me curious about the text, about the author, and about what was going on in the world when Warren wrote the book. It never occurred to me how she did it.

Since the time when my own educational career ended, I've occasionally been asked to teach or provide a guest lecture. Thinking back to the most compelling teachers I'd had in college and the most dynamic lectures I'd attended, I often started from the premise that I had to make the material entertaining. A colleague of mine was so good at weaving imagery and words together in a presentation (I was in awe of his skill) that I assumed this was the model. I thought that by somehow surrounding what you are trying to teach with a package that is so interesting, shiny, and clever, kids will be rapt and somehow give you their undivided attention!

While there are those who can somehow pull this off, I've been unable to. Trying to teach like this has been like trying to power a big boat, needing an ever bigger motor in the form of better presentations, ideas, jokes, and gimmicks. I can produce some interesting tales and get some laughs with some self-deprecating humor, but I typically left my own performances wondering if I'd made an impression—If I'd drawn anyone in. I thought I needed a bigger motor. But watching Ramsey's class, I began to feel there might be a different model.

Part of my failing here, in retrospect, is that I am incredibly curious about the world and assume that everyone else is, too. I think everyone has the capacity for curiosity, but not everyone is as automatically driven by it as I am. I love to learn how something works or how to do something. One friend referred to it as "Third Chapter Syndrome." You get to chapter three, see what it's all about, and move on. Another friend called me a dilettante. I thought he meant frivolous, so I had to look it up. Most usage today is derogatory: "someone who cultivates an interest without real commitment or knowledge." But there was a time when it meant something different. Back in the age of discovery, a dilettante was actually "a devoted amateur." I'm pretty sure my friend was taking a pot shot—I had been telling him about how much fun I was having trying to learn to play the piano while at the same time trying to teach myself how to code in C—but that's how I am. A long time ago I realized I wouldn't be the best at anything because my interests were too varied. BUT I could get good at a bunch of stuff because I'm so curious!

Ramsey's TED Talk struck a chord with me. It was like lifting the veil on my own natural curiosity, but also on how I had failed in my own efforts to teach. And you can see how Ramsey's own curiosity drives him. But it's not just curiosity; there's also a bias to action which, in combination, creates a powerful duo. Ramsey was gearing up to teach robotics at Sonoma Academy for the first time and was sharing some of the project structure with me. I made a suggestion about trying to isolate the challenge to what he was trying to teach and use shortcuts for everything else. Specifically, I suggested using LEGOs as the construction medium since he was more interested in teaching kids how to make something that ran their programming rather than how to become expert fabricators. What struck me about Ramsey was that when he shared the course outline a day later, he'd already incorporated the LEGO idea. His ability to synthesize information and apply it immediately struck me. I'm much more contemplative and like to do a lot of weighing before making a decision.

This bias towards action reminded me of a friend who is an expert fabricator. Instead of making copious drawings or studies or spending time analyzing (as I would do), he would just start building with only the most basic of sketches. The first attempt usually evolved quite a bit and ended up being the prototype for the second (or even third) attempt of the same thing. What's surprising is that by the time he had finished his second or sometimes third and final iteration, I would still have been thinking about my first cut. What is it that keeps us from trying something out immediately? Why wait?

In the pages that follow, Ramsey provides a different model for teaching, incorporating the power of curiosity with a bias towards action. I recently spent some time in a classroom with Ramsey and was blown away by the energy in the class. The kids were at it— teaching themselves, it seemed. They were showing me the things they were prototyping: an autonomously driving RC car, a free-space laser music link, a proximity-detecting Bluetooth mailbox unlocker … I leaned over to Ramsey and asked, "How much of this stuff do you understand regarding how they did it?" to which Ramsey replied, "Almost nothing!"

If my old model of teaching was the mega powerboat trying to plow through a stiff current with a *ginormous* motor, Ramsey's model of getting curiosity on your side makes it more like sailing. You just have to raise a big enough sail—something to catch kids' curiosity—and suddenly the class is propelling itself. With fingertips on the tiller and the sheet, you are steering a massive vessel at a blistering clip.

THE SPARK

Can we be the surgeons of our classrooms—
as if what we are doing will one day save
lives? Our students are worth it, and each
case is different.

—*"3 RULES TO SPARK LEARNING,"* **4:48**

SIX CENTIMETERS. As a high school chemistry teacher, I am very familiar with this measurement. It's about the width of a dollar bill, the length of a typical human thumb, approximately two small paper clips laid end to end, and the measurement of an assortment of other random items that we chemistry teachers have students compare when trying to inspire an appreciation for the metric system. A typical struggle, unit conversions. We look for significant figures, accuracy, precision … blah, blah, blah.

In May of 2008, my familiarity with this metric distance took a much more serious form. After switching healthcare providers, my new physician suggested that I receive an echocardiogram to test for any negative effects caused by the appearance of mild high blood pressure. While the results detected no damage, the scan did show something unexpected: a large aneurysm at the base of my thoracic aorta—six centimeters, to be precise. In the first vessel blood passes through after leaving the heart, a diameter of 3.5 centimeters defines a healthy size of this region commonly referred to as the "aortic root." The aneurysm measured six centimeters, almost double the healthy size. Suddenly the significant figures, which once dominated the more banal side of my lesson process, assumed a significant role.

And so began a two-year journey as my wife and I were referred to different doctors and surveyed various surgical procedures, all while trying to enjoy the birth of our first child and preparing for the arrival of our second. After weighing our options, we eventually decided on a relatively new type of open-heart surgery that would not require the placement of a mechanical aortic heart valve to repair the aneurysm. At the age of thirty-six, the reality of a lifetime of blood thinning medication and the inevitable risk of infection made the new procedure worth the gamble. The surgery was ultimately a huge success, and today the weight of the significance of "six centimeters," once a heavy boulder on my back, feels more like a small pebble in my pocket. An experience I'm only reminded of when I see the faint scar on my chest in the bathroom mirror or while swimming on the beach with my children.

After the "poor me" phase passed, what fascinated me most was not the intricacies of cardiovascular physiology, the mechanics of the surgery, or the chemistry of Dacron, the substance that would ultimately be used to replace my aneurysm. The teacher in me was drawn to the mindset of my surgeon. His confidence. His faith in his ability to fix the problem. His almost nonchalant approach to describing the nearly five hours that my heart would be stopped while he operated.

His mentality and the comfort his confidence provided mesmerized me. Where did he get such confidence? How dare he be so certain about something so seemingly scary? The audacity! How did he get so good at it and have so much skill in something where the risks were so high? Whatever training methods were used in his education and whatever pedagogy his teachers employed to instill such a sense of confidence in him must have worked—really well! I wanted to know about his teachers. I wanted to be that kind of teacher for my students. I wondered, *Could I be the surgeon of my classroom?*

As I recovered and prepared to go back to the classroom in the fall, I gathered my notes and tried to isolate what it was about the doctor and his approach to my surgery that so impressed me. I wanted to make sense of it so I could share it with my students. I had spent the previous years behaving more like an entertainer than an educator. Crippled by a fear of being "boring," I had been exploiting my knowledge of chemistry to be a magician, using demonstrations and explosions to gain student popularity all while luring students into listening to another boring lecture.

This flip was hardly innovative. It was more like a cheap attempt at being "innovative" without truly facing my real issues as a teacher.

The sequence went something like this: Homework, practice, Explosion! Boring lecture. Repeat. Sure, sometimes the "lecture" was packaged into a video, but this flip was hardly innovative. It was more like a cheap attempt at being "innovative" without truly facing my real issues as a teacher. Generally speaking, my class was "popular" with students. And why not? They liked the explosions.

With the advent of Google Docs came the ability to solicit student feedback about my teaching. It was a mistake not to ask for the students' names on my first survey using a Google Form. However, this careless mistake—made just five days before my surgery—proved strikingly serendipitous and, ultimately, very purposeful!

AP Chemistry Honest Feedback Form

*Required

Please provide me with your HONEST feedback about AP Chemistry this year.*

[Submit]

Never submit passwords through Google Forms.

Allowing the students to respond to the survey anonymously led to a barrage of honest feedback that corroborated the nagging voice I had tried to ignore. Those responses confirmed what I had suspected: My first ten years in the classroom were more like a phase of "pseudoteaching" rather than inspiring instruction from a teacher worthy of being "popular." I'd been doing the type of teaching that made it easy to pat myself on the back because students were begging to transfer into my class. It had become all too easy to ignore the strong discrepancies between students truly understanding content and simply being entertained. Reading their survey responses was at once enlightening and brutal.

5/2/2010 8:48:48	It seemed, to be perfectly honest, that you were experimenting on us ... I HATE it when the problem looks different on a test. Stop trying to be all creative and stuff.
5/2/2010 8:47:30	I LOOOOOVED watching you blow stuff up, but I still don't have a clue what stoichiometry is.
5/2/2010 8:49:31	Even though I'm not planning on studying science AT ALL in college, your class was the only one I looked forward to this year.
5/2/2010 8:48:02	...not sure what all this stuff means, but I got an A, so I guess I do. I consider you a friend.

Of all the comments, it is the last one shown that really stung: "... not sure what this stuff means, but I got an A so I guess I do. I consider you a friend." In one moment of honest, anonymous feedback, this student called into question my ability to facilitate an understanding of chemistry and assess that understanding. It is incredible how one sentence can pack such a punch!

The answers I had culled regarding the source of my surgeon's skill and demeanor didn't come right away. The answers were diluted over casual appointments during CT exam follow-ups, emails, and kind, personal phone calls I knew I received only because of my unique situation. With each meeting, email, or call, my anxiety transformed into curiosity about the procedure he would eventually, confidently perform.

As my stamina returned to normal and my chest began to heal, the fall of the 2010 school year approached, and I felt an overwhelming desire to improve myself as a teacher. I wanted to make the A referenced above have meaning. I needed to ground "stoichiometry" in the package of conceptual beauty that it is: The field of chemistry that empowers the synthesized medicines, drugs, food, etc., with amazing precision. And just as importantly, I wanted to make my class more than just explosions; I wanted to establish my relationships with my students in the beautiful content we were exploring first. How could I do this?

I wanted to make my class more than just explosions; I wanted to establish my relationships with my students in the beautiful content we were exploring first.

When I took the time to reflect on my surgeon's words and messages, three themes continued to appear. First, it was clear that he was incredibly curious not only about open heart surgery, but also about the specific procedure I was going to have. He spoke about the intricacies of the aortic valve with the excitement of a young child talking about their first LEGO set. Mid-conversation he would get out a piece of paper and begin to draw the various forms of the procedure. What's more, he encouraged me to be just as curious. To seek information about what was happening inside my body. To conduct Google searches about it. To read about it. To learn about it. It was clear that my surgeon thrived in the space between knowing and not knowing everything about my specific condition. Could he repair my aneurysm without the need for a mechanical heart valve and blood-thinning medication? From my perspective, his tireless efforts to answer this question, more than anything, seemed to define his vocation.

Second, it was obvious from our conversations that trial—and unfortunately error—were central to the surgery I would have. My procedure was performed at Kaiser San Francisco, although after my diagnosis two years prior, my doctor referred me to Stanford University for a consultation regarding a more complex but more tested surgery. He wanted me to know what options were available, but he also expressed hesitation and told me he was working on a new, simpler procedure that, once he had performed it enough times, would be better suited for my specific condition. Again, his calmness and sense of confidence blew my mind! Underneath his words lay the reality that even heart surgery was a skill to be mastered. Despite his confidence, that trial and error lasted up until a few hours before anesthesia. And just in case things didn't go to plan, I signed a consent form allowing him to place a mechanical heart valve if necessary. Nothing is immune to disorder, to entropy, to mess. It was obvious he had learned to embrace the unavoidable process of revision as essential, powerful, and difficult.

Lastly, he often discussed his constant collaboration with colleagues at other universities and hospitals who were equally passionate about similar procedures. He spoke about his time as a surgical resident at Baylor University and about his colleagues in Florida who had performed the same procedure for which I was scheduled. His comments were always undergirded with a deep sense of reflective practice. It was clear that he was part of a community of learners who were all accessing, sharing, and revising procedures to better serve their patients. Although not unexpected in a vocation where the stakes are as high as surgery, it was comforting to know that a community of physicians spent time reflecting on how best to serve me. And it was through this powerful, cumulative reflection of a strong community that my procedure was designed and would eventually be performed.

Those three themes—curiosity, disorder, and reflection—were the simple yet powerful constructs which provided meaning during the most difficult and uncertain period in my life. Three things about which I am confident my surgeon has no idea resonated with me. Three things that provided the rules I needed to step back into the classroom committed to being a better teacher—to be "popular" for the right reasons and to treat my students and the subject I teach as if they will save lives.

When I entered the classroom that fall, I reflected on this experience and scribbled down three rules on the front page of my lesson-planning book. I promised myself that I would not leave my classroom until my lesson plan for the next day embodied some aspect of each rule. Here is what I wrote:

Rule #1: Curiosity comes first—I will try my best to spark authentic student questioning before delivering content.

Rule #2: Embrace the mess—I will try my best to build a structure that leverages trial and error.

Rule #3: Practice reflection—I will try my best to view each lesson plan as fluid and deserving of revision.

Spark Learning shares my journey from "pseudoteaching" to an instructional approach that places those three rules before anything else because they are the key to unlocking and harnessing the power of student curiosity. This book traces my journey into a world where student questions, the mess of learning, and the art of revision are seen as symbiotic entities capable of building mastery in both the teacher and student. It is, if you will, my post-surgery teaching manifesto.

In the chapters that follow, I will attempt to unpack each rule through a lens of the philosophical and the tangible by sharing specific classroom examples, technology tutorials, stories, reflections, opinions, research, and workbook space for your own lesson design. Teaching is a beautifully complex, personal, and difficult art that demands authenticity and extreme passion.

I am not pretending to have all the answers. I don't possess a "Silver Bullet," nor am I challenging the myriad of other approaches that so many fellow educators have found successful. At times the methods in this book will mirror those of a workshop, and at other times, a reflection on teaching. Once in a while (more frequently than I would like) the book takes a peek into the mind of an obsessed workaholic who takes himself and his career way too seriously (only half-joking).

In short, the pages that follow are my personal reflections into a process that has brought incredible meaning to the art of teaching—for me. The stars aligned one day, and I was able to share six minutes of my story on a stage with many, many others. This book quenches my thirst to share more than six minutes with you. And as my good friend and fellow educator Adam Bellow says, "Doing something awesome as a teacher and not sharing it is just selfish." I'm taking his advice. Thank you for joining me!

RULE #1:
CURIOSITY
COMES FIRST

Questions can be windows into great
instruction but not the other way around.
— *"3 Rules to Spark Learning,"* 4:09

THINK FOR A MOMENT about a time when you were really curious about something. Perhaps it was what the next episode of your favorite show or the final page of a great book would reveal. Or maybe it was that I've-got-to-find-the-answer feeling you get when you just can't remember the tune to a song long forgotten. Or perhaps, like my surgeon, you want to improve upon a complex process. For him, it was open-heart surgery. For you, that curiosity may have to do with baking, wood working, coding—or teaching.

Regardless of the source, these curiosity "sparks" share one thing in common: the presence of an information gap—a space of missing content that spans directly between knowing and not knowing. It's an invisible cognitive barrier separating frustration and reward. On the surface, the emotional benefit we get from closing the information gap seems like a simple phenomenon, a fleeting feeling so intertwined into how we live our lives each day that we rarely take the time to contemplate or, even better, leverage its unseen power.

Current research reveals that the emotion of being curious is something more than a quest for missing information. Curiosity transcends our ingrained image of a silly monkey who gets into trouble, and redefines this journey into something very cerebral: the anticipation of a cognitive reward. This anticipation is so intense that, once curiosity is piqued, our minds are strengthened, connections are made, and awareness is enhanced. Throughout the process, our subconscious mind prepares to help us fill the information gap. In short, the power of curiosity is not found when the desire for information is quenched; instead, it is the presence of the unknown that has the power to build our mental muscle. Curiosity empowers humans to negotiate complexity by priming the brain's need to learn with all its vigor.

Science's relatively new understanding of curiosity has inspired researchers to investigate the ways in which information gaps prepare the brain for learning. In a landmark study at the University of California Davis, neuroscientist Charan Ranganath and his team asked nineteen participants to review more than one hundred questions, rating each in terms of how curious they were about the answer. Following their rating of curiosity, each subject revisited the questions while Ranganath and his team scanned their brain activity using functional magnetic resonance imaging (fMRI). During the scanning session participants would view a question, then wait fourteen seconds and view a photograph of a face totally unrelated to the trivia before seeing the answer.

Upon conclusion of the scans, the team tested participants to see how well they could recall and retain both the trivia answers and the faces they had seen. The research revealed, with statistical significance, that participant curiosity in a question would predict not only better memory for the answer to the question but also, fascinatingly, memory for the unrelated face that had preceded it. Translation: When you are curious about something, your learning improves. In fact, when you are curious, you can learn anything more easily.

Research conducted by Williams College Psychologist Nate Kornell confirms the findings by Ranganath that curiosity can supercharge our ability to negotiate complexity. In a study published in the Journal of Psychological Science, Kornell asked participants to review a list of words printed in fonts of varying sizes and predicted how likely they would be to remember them on a later test. As predicted, participants indicated

---

Once curiosity is piqued, our minds are strengthened, connections are made, and awareness is enhanced.

---

that they were most confident in their ability to remember words in large print, rating font size as more likely to sustain memory even more than repeated practice. After testing participant hypothesis on follow-up tests, the study proved exactly the opposite. Font size made no difference, and practice paid off.

Kornell's research directly challenges the relationship between difficulty and learning. According to Kornell, "If you study something twice, in spaced sessions, it's harder to process the material the second time, and people think it's counterproductive. But the opposite is true: You learn more, even though it feels harder. Fluency is playing a trick on judgment." And perhaps, on a larger scale, findings such as these allude to a much more important "trick" that can potentially have huge implications on teaching and learning:

1. Curiosity doesn't always feel good when defined as an information gap.

2. Entertainment is not the same thing as engagement.

Although there can be a thin line between curiosity and entertainment, our cognitive architecture is strengthened by the latter. As Kornell so eloquently states: "Difficulty builds mental muscle, while ease builds only confidence."

Keeping the above research in mind, it is easy to see how, if leveraged appropriately, information gaps can be powerful tools for educators. If indeed the mere awareness of an information gap builds "mental muscle," sparking a sense of curiosity should be central to any teacher's box of strategies. What could be more important to educators than empowering their students to negotiate complexity with efficiency, skill, and confidence? Although a compelling argument, marketing curiosity as an instructional tool to teachers can be a challenging sell. Our relationships with information are central to how we define our work, and regardless of subject, transferring information to students encapsulates much of the teaching profession. If it is, instead, the awareness of missing information—not the delivery of information—that empowers students to learn, what then is the role of the teacher? After all, *wanting* information is not the same thing as *having* information.

Having spent much of my time since my surgery reflecting on authentic student motivation and the tension alluded to above between wanting and having information, I have come to the understanding that being curious about knowledge and having knowledge are not separate entities but a symbiotic pair. The *wanting* and the *having* of knowledge acts like a "dynamic duo" of pedagogy with a sequencing that is key to meaningful learning and instruction. To better explain this instructional pairing, it is helpful to look at a plot of "Curiosity versus Confidence" where confidence in a subject is correlated to having knowledge about that topic.

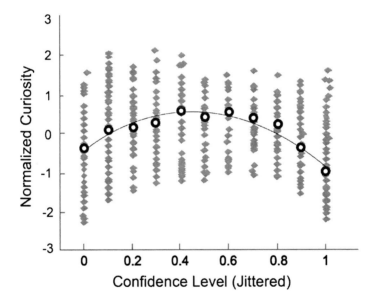

Figure 1.1

Corroborating the "information gap" hypothesis that a feeling of curiosity is related to the absence—not the presence—of information, the inverted U-shaped curve shown above provides additional information about the parameters of the information gap. That is, when confidence or knowledge in a topic is low, curiosity is low, and when knowledge in a topic is high, curiosity is also low. However there is a "sweet spot" where just enough information is provided to create maximum curiosity. As movie producer and writer J.J. Abrams so eloquently stated in his TED Talk, "The Mystery Box": "The withholding of information ... is much more engaging ... you love it because you don't hear it."

Recalling the research by both Charan Ranganath and Nate Kornell, not only do you "love" the information more when you are curious, but you are more capable of processing the intricacies and complexities of that information. The graph below demonstrates the relationship between the "mental muscle," alluded to by Kornell, and curiosity by plotting accuracy of response to questions versus participant curiosity in the same questions.

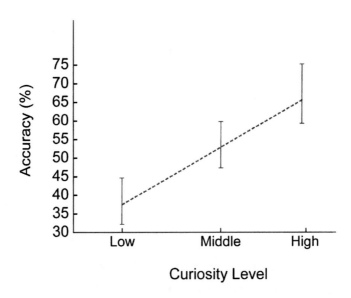

Figure 1.2

Both the inverted-U graph and the above graph provide clarity to a major paradox in the curiosity research literature: It is through the withholding, rather than providing, of information that our cognition strengthened. Despite this fact, our responsibility as educators is to find the "sweet spot," where just enough information is removed to peak curiosity and strengthen mental muscle, all while not demotivating students—a difficult but worthy task. I believe that the art of teaching lies in this challenge to sequence instruction placing curiosity first. We must prime the brain for meaningful learning, withhold information, and then deliver information. It is this pedagogical combination that can make all the difference in a student's authentic understanding of and interest in a topic. From my perspective as a curious patient, it is this combination that empowered my surgeon's lifesaving skills.

As teachers, it is not enough to simply have an understanding of the research regarding cognitive mechanisms or curiosity. We must also strive to bridge the gap between a graphical representation of curiosity and exactly how to position each of our students on a living axis within the information-gap sweet spot. Of particular use to educators is a construct referred to as "Involuntary Curiosity." Described in the research literature as the "unintentional awareness of an information gap caused by exposure to curiosity-inducing stimuli," the "unintentional" portion of Involuntary Curiosity nicely overlaps with the realities of the average student in the United States. We cannot hide from the fact that school is a requirement of being a young citizen in our country. Yes, it is an honor, right, and even a blessing. But it is also a requirement.

Whether or not it is true, I always enter each day of class with the cynical assumption that my students do not want to be there. I assume that it is my responsibility to engage and motivate them through the way I position the content—through information I withhold and provide. It is my job, therefore, to make the information gap salient—visible and tangible—in order to build mental muscle. While I am hopeful that many of my students intentionally crave the problem-solving process and are naturally curious about chemistry, the art of teaching, for me, lies in this challenge. I realize that in this assumption I've taken a controversial stance, one that some might call a negative perspective on teaching. Despite the negative aspects of this assumption, it is a position that helps me transform what I do each day from a job into a vocation. *Can I create a spontaneous, authentic sense of inquiry in my students for each topic of study?* This question drives me!

Let's go back to the research for a moment. The literature on Involuntary Curiosity discusses many ways to spark that curiosity; however, only three strategies are particularly applicable for the classroom teacher. The three curiosity "sparks" listed below should be implemented with the goal of positioning students directly in that sweet spot where a strategic amount of information is withheld and maximum mental muscle is exercised. This is the first point of contact in the dynamic duo of presenting and then quenching an information gap. Doing this well is an art that undoubtedly will take any educator a career to master.

Spark #1: Missing Information

Description: Provide students with an artifact that has information strategically removed.

Goal: Spark questioning about essential elements of the topic.

Spark #2: Anticipated Solution

Description: Provide students with an artifact, usually an audio or video clip that ends early.

Goal: Spark questioning about how the clip will resolve.

Spark #3: Surprising Result

Description: Provide students with an artifact, usually an image, video clip, or reading in which the result is surprising, perplexing, or shocking.

Goal: Spark questioning in search of more details that explain the phenomena.

Appropriately, my entry into sparking Involuntary Curiosity did not come from a page in my lesson-planning book but from a very observant and gutsy student named Kevin. My first week back after surgery, I began my sophomore chemistry class as I did every year with a simple lesson on the scientific method and chemical-versus-physical changes. I decided that, before jumping into my new-and-improved lesson-planning agenda, I would warm up slowly and leverage the same sequence of instruction that "worked" last school year:

PHASE 1: Lecture—What are the characteristics of chemical reactions?

PHASE 2: Lab—What will happen when you put a candle under a jar?

PHASE 3: Extension—What will happen if you put your candle under a different-sized jar?

I loved this introductory activity. It included a clear lecture that provided a solid framework for designing an experiment, recording data, and testing variables. Add to that a simple lab process—involving fire!—with a factor that can be easily manipulated: the amount of oxygen inside of the jar. From elementary school students to graduate school students to the random person walking down the street, when questioned about why the candle goes out when placed under a jar, nearly every person responds, seemingly reflexively, with the same answer. You're probably thinking of that answer right now: *The candle uses up all of the oxygen in the jar.*

While this response contains some correct information, the phenomena of a candle going out under a jar is much more complex and, as I would soon find out, extremely misrepresented in my chemistry curriculum. I followed the lab with another short lecture during which I told students exactly what they thought they knew: there is no more oxygen left in the jar. Much like the typical responses alluded to above, this information was essentially derived from my gut. A reflex blindly grounded in a misconception rather than in a strong foundation in chemistry.

"I don't believe you."

The words rang loud immediately after I concluded my lecture. The bold statement made Kevin, a sophomore, who normally sat quietly in the back of the class, appear to be an intellectual giant. An intimidating figure whose food was my "Imposter Complex" and whose goal was to prove me wrong.

"Excuse me?" I said with a hint of insecurity.

The class looked back at Kevin. Then back at me. Then back at Kevin.

"I don't believe you. I don't think it's that simple. I think there is still oxygen in the jar."

The class looked at me. Then back at Kevin. Then back at me. A number of potential responses to Kevin ran through my head:

Actually Kevin, it does use up all the oxygen. But we can talk more about it after class.

Why don't you go ahead and email me your question so we can discuss it later.

Would anybody like to help Kevin understand why the candle does use up all of the oxygen in the jar?

As I cycled through each insecure rebuttal, I felt more and more like a fraud. I was convinced he, and the entire class for that matter, believed that I had *Chemistry for Dummies* in my bag with frantic highlights and notes scribbled all over it. Did they know that I was only a high school chemistry teacher because I didn't get into medical school like I had initially planned? I was suddenly sure they knew that my lowest score on each of the two MCAT examinations I took (and failed) were on the Chemistry section and that my major was actually biology, and chemistry was simply the only job that was open at the time of my hiring. I was confident they knew all of this. They had figured it out: I was an impostor, a fraud!

Just as the mouth of the impostor (my mouth) began to open and rattle off some tired, typical, hierarchical teacher response like "I have a tie and you don't," I was struck with a different option. This new reply grew out of my summer of existential reflection about my role as a teacher. I'm not exactly sure where the two words came from, but looking back, I now recognize that they are the two words that sparked a new phase in my career: "Prove it."

Immediately after these words emerged from my mouth, the vibe in the classroom changed. Kevin no longer was the seven-foot intellectual giant he had appeared to be seconds earlier, and the students no longer seemed to be stuck between the dichotomy of his intelligence and my oblivion. And best of all, I didn't feel like an impostor anymore.

"Prove it."

In a voice that had transformed in tone from intimidating to curious, Kevin said, "Instead of putting one candle under different-sized jars, I noticed some rubber stoppers on the table. I grabbed one and put one candle on top of the rubber stopper (Image 1.1). Then I lit them both and put the jar on top of them. When one was higher than the other, the top one went out first under the jar (Image 1.2). The bottom one stays lit for way longer!"

"Show us, Kevin!" I said in an equally curious tone that seemed to calm my students and build curiosity in everybody. I grabbed my phone and shot a video of Kevin's ingenious system.

Image 1.1

Image 1.2

It was as if Kevin had sensed the direction I wanted to go as a teacher and had kindly (if somewhat intimidatingly) given me the push I needed to make the subtle yet significant change in my lesson-planning process. It was the first rule: Place curiosity first. The subsequent mess would follow as students hustled to try new methods and challenge old paradigms. So be it. We would all deviate from the script and be empowered by the process of reflection. In fact, Kevin's experiment provided our class with a perfect example of the "Surprising Result" Involuntary Curiosity can spark. Suddenly a powerful window had been flung open and curiosity flooded in as the entire class began to investigate the chemistry of a burning candle.

IDEAS FOR SPARKING INVOLUNTARY CURIOSITY

You can create similar discovery experiences in your classroom using the three sparks of Missing Information, Anticipated Solution, and Surprising Result. No matter what grade level or subject area you teach, these sparks can ignite curiosity in your students. The following pages provide three different, specific lesson-planning examples for each type of Involuntary Curiosity spark previously discussed. The examples are not meant to be comprehensive. Rather, they serve as models for you as you begin to curate media artifacts and plan your own curiosity sparks. Each example begins by noting the academic subject and specific topic that the spark is geared toward. The examples move on to include images and descriptions of the media artifact(s) used to spark student questioning about the specific topic. Finally, implementation instructions, logic, and specific technology tutorials are provided. I am hopeful that the example lesson-starters that follow, although science and math related, will provide you with a tangible template for strategies around sparking Involuntary Curiosity in students.

Spark #1: Missing Information

1. Subject—History

2. Topic—Civil Rights

3. Artifact

Shown below are two different Word Clouds. Word Clouds are Data Visualizations which depict groupings of words from a piece of text with high frequency words shown larger than low frequency words. Image 1.3 (below) is a visualization of Martin Luther King's "I Have a Dream" speech. Image 1.4 (to the right) is a visualization derived from Barack Obama's 2008 speech, "A More Perfect Union." This pairing of images represents a "missing information" curiosity spark in that the associated text for each visualization is not noted. (See page 124 for more info about leveraging Word Clouds as a learning tool.)

Image 1.3

Image 1.4

4. Instructions

Explain and model what a Word Cloud is, using a random piece of text of your choosing. Show each visualization above side-by-side to students prior to investigating the topic in class. Ask students to view the visualizations individually. Observe closely to see if questions emerge from students naturally. If questions do not emerge, ask, "What questions do you have?" Desired student questions include the following:

- Are the Word Clouds from different speeches?

- Did the Word Clouds come from a similar period in American History?

- Does each Word Cloud address racial equality in America?

5. Logic

Students may be able to deduce from the high frequency words in each visualization that they are from speeches related to civil rights and racial equality in America. After revealing the Missing Information (identity of each speech), a student-catalyzed discussion about similarities and differences between each speech can emerge, eventually leading to a discussion and subsequent lesson on Civil Rights and racial equality in America today, and over time.

6. Technology and Tutorial

- Google (google.com)
- Word Sift (wordsift.com)

Step 1: Conduct a Google search for Martin Luther King's "I Have a Dream" speech.

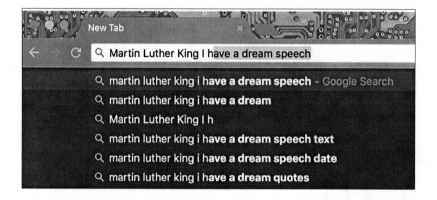

Step 2: Copy and paste the text from the speech into Word Sift and click "Sift."

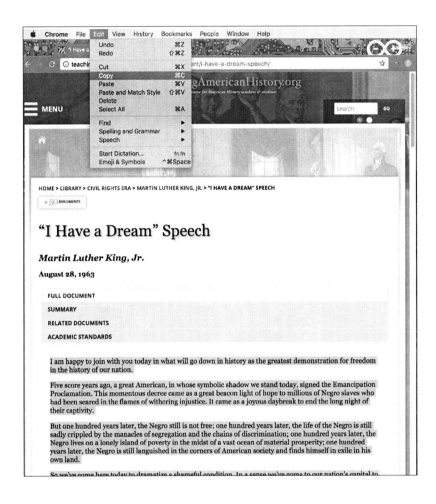

Step 3: Repeat Process with Barack Obama's "A More Perfect Union" speech.

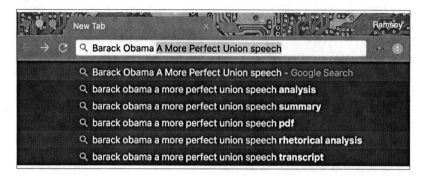

CURIOSITY SPARKED?
Here's a space to jot down your ideas.

Spark #2: Anticipated Solution

1. Subject—Physical Science

2. Topic—Mass, Volume, and Density

3. Artifact

The image below is a recreation of the opening scene to the movie *Raiders of the Lost Ark* where Indiana Jones is attempting to steal a pure-gold statue by replacing it with a bag of sand of equal weight. Although the artifact below depicts an image, I have found that showing a video clip, trimmed strategically to only show Indiana (a) preparing the bag of sand, and (b) making the switch to be much more engaging. This artifact represents an "anticipated solution" spark, in that it is edited to end prior to resolution of the scene.

4. Instructions

Obtain *Raiders of the Lost Ark* on Google Play, iTunes, or the video interface of choice. Display only the scene shown in the image for students prior to beginning a unit in mass, volume, and density. The scene occurs between 7:47 and 8:01 when watching the version from Google Play. Stop the clip just after Indiana swaps the golden idol for the bag of sand, but before it is revealed whether or not his exchange was successful. After playing the clip, listen for any questions that naturally emerge from students. If no one volunteers a question, ask, "What questions do you have about this video clip?" Alternatively, I have found the question, "What mistake is Indiana making?" to work well in funneling students to the difference between mass and volume. Desired questions include the following:

- Shouldn't the bag be much bigger?
- Is that statue pure gold?
- Does he think all things with the same size have the same weight?

5. Logic

Because Indiana is attempting to replace a statue that is assumed to be pure gold with a bag of sand of roughly equal volume, he assumes that all things with the same size have the same mass. By ending the clip before the scene is resolved, students can anticipate the resolution and determine "how big" the bag of sand should have been. What follows will be a student-catalyzed lesson about mass, volume, and density. Although a fictitious scenario, the scene forces students to confront misconceptions around mass and volume. The analogous situation can be replicated easily using sand and various solid-metal objects.

6. Technology

- Google (google.com)
- Google Play (play.google.com)

Spark #3: Surprising Result

1. Subject—Algebra

2. Topic—Linear Equations

3. Artifact

Use the image below and the statement: "When you look at the stars, you are looking into the past!" This artifact and statement combination cause intrigue and yield a "surprising result."

When you look at the stars, you are looking into the past!

4. Instructions

Display image to students and read the intriguing question above prior to beginning the unit on linear equations. If questions do not emerge, ask, "What questions do you have about this statement?" Desired questions include the following:

- How far away is the closest star?

- How fast does light travel?
- Are we looking into the past when we look at the moon or just the stars?

5. Logic

The presence of light from the sky, be it from the moon, planets, or stars, is something all students have experienced as a common part of daily life. As such, the statement, "When you look at the stars, you are looking into the past!" is surprising and can create an immediate sense of cognitive dissonance. The tension between the way students perceive the world and the way it actually operates can make an information gap noticeable and spark a moment of Involuntary Curiosity. After a discussion of the speed of light, students can attempt to solve for the time it takes light to reach a viewer on Earth from the moon, stars, etc. Ideally a student-catalyzed lesson will surface about linear equations, specifically distance = rate x time.

6. Technology and Tutorial

- Google Advanced Image Search

Step 1: Do a search for "Stars" on Google Advanced Image Search.

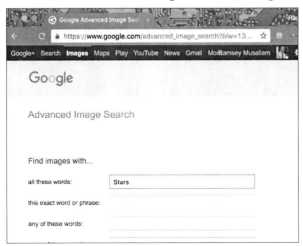

Step 2: Choose "Free to use or share, even commercially" from the Usage Rights dropdown menu.

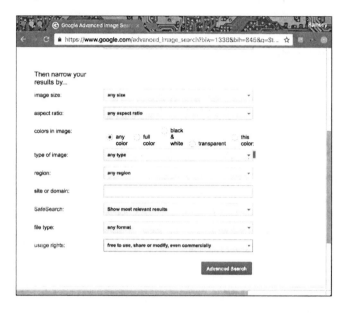

Step 3: Choose the image you like, right click on it, and select "Save Image As."

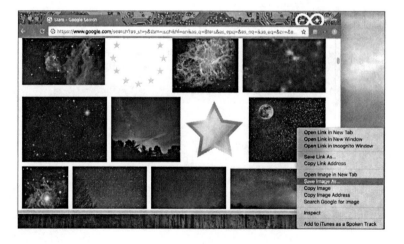

The Art of Sparking Creativity

Whenever I share my passion for leveraging such strategies with fellow teachers, inevitably the following question surfaces: "How do you find your curiosity-sparking artifacts?" The pedagogical logic behind sparking student curiosity always resonates with my colleagues, but finding and modifying media artifacts that can effectively make an information gap visible can seem intimidating.

My response to this question is always twofold. First, my answer deals with instruction and planning. I understand that placing the task of sparking student curiosity before the transfer of information presents a new challenge to the teacher as the designer of the lesson. Most teachers are familiar with the process of working with the end in mind to design instruction that achieves certain academic outcomes (such as meeting standards or doing well on assessments). In some ways, designing lessons with the intent of sparking curiosity is similar. Still, it requires a paradigm shift that presents its own challenge with respect to lesson-plan organization. That shift, moving from designing instruction to creating situations where students desire instruction, is subtle but very different philosophically. It's a flip that requires teachers to behave more like artists than planners. This perspective, in my opinion, transforms the way we, as teachers, see the world. It adds a new level of joy, creativity, and passion to our vocation. Whenever I see something on the Internet that intrigues me, or spot a movie or news clip that begs a question, or stumble across something interesting in the physical world, I always ask myself: Can this artifact be modified to spark student curiosity?

In the past, these same kinds of events seemed ordinary and never stood out as moments that could transform my teaching. But my focus on creating opportunities for curiosity in the classroom colors all I see in the world with a layer of instructional design! Just yesterday I stepped out of the movie theatre in the middle of watching The Martian because I just had to jot down ways I could leverage a specific scene to spark curiosity in my chemistry class. Ideas are everywhere, which is why the first piece of advice I give teachers who struggle with finding curiosity-sparking artifacts is to simply look around. Be aware of the world around you; it will present you with an endless surplus of artifacts to spark student curiosity. Just watch.

Ideas are everywhere ....
Just watch.

The second part of my answer deals with the technological aspect of gathering media for curiosity-sparking lesson starters. Once artifacts are found, it is essential to have a system for capturing and storing them in a central location that is well organized and available to other educators. Most importantly, the system for saving artifacts must be simple and require minimal effort. I have explored many ways of collecting and storing ideas, including bookmarking websites, using notepad features on my mobile device to store ideas, and even writing down websites and video titles in a physical notebook. Each of the methods I just described, and a myriad of other random systems I hacked together in the past, did their job, but they never seemed to have the combination of simplicity and efficacy I was looking for. Then I discovered two applications: If This Then That and Pocket.

If This Then That (ifttt.com) allows the user to combine online applications such as YouTube, Google Drive, Dropbox, Blogger, Facebook, Twitter, etc., and create "Applets." Applets are triggers that connect two different applications in a causal fashion to create an outcome. For example, an Applet could be: "IF I post a tweet, THEN post the tweet to

Facebook." The options with If This Then That are seemingly endless, and upon first investigation the application intimidated me with all its variations and potential uses. Then an idea struck me: I could use If This Then That to create a trigger that automatically stored media artifacts!

To create the triggers, I first limited the online artifacts I would use to pictures and videos. With respect to videos, I gave myself permission to only use YouTube as the media outlet. This decision allowed me to create a powerful trigger for capturing and organizing curiosity sparks: IF I like a video on YouTube, THEN add the video link to a row in a Google Drive sheet. This trigger allows me to simply hit the "thumbs up" button on any YouTube video on my computer or mobile device to shuttle the video link and description to a row in a Google Drive sheet. Because the information is now in Google Drive, I can share the sheet with my colleagues or even on my blog to spread the curiosity-sparking love! Once a week, I visit the spreadsheet and reflect on the videos I have stored and choose an applicable clip to begin editing for Involuntary Curiosity sparks.

If This Then That
Tutorial for Saving Videos

The screenshots below outline the process of setting up this Applet.

Step 1: Create an account at ifttt.com and then click on "New Applet." On the Applet Maker page, click on "+ this."

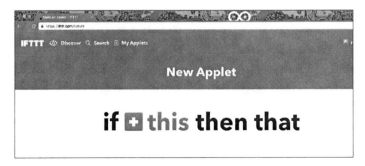

Step 2: Choose the service you want to use as your trigger. In this case we'll use YouTube as the trigger. If this is your first time using IFTTT and YouTube together, follow the on-screen instructions to allow IFTTT permission to connect with your YouTube account. (*Note:* You will need a YouTube account for this to work.)

Step 3: Click on "New liked video" to set the trigger.

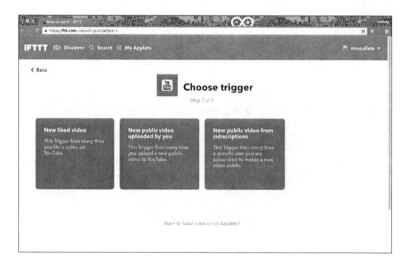

Step 4: Next, click on "+ that" to set the outcome you want.

Step 5: Select Google Drive from the service options. (Again, you'll have to allow permission to connect the services if this is the first time you've used this Google Drive with IFTTT.)

Step 6: Click "Add row to spreadsheet." The next screen will allow you to name the spreadsheet and your desired file location on Google Drive. Click on "Create Action." The final screen on IFTTT will allow you to review the trigger you've created. Click "Finish" to complete the process.

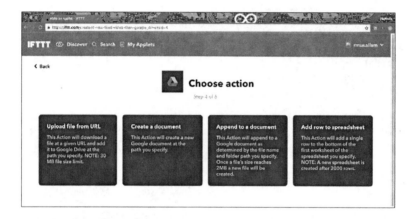

Step 7: Go to YouTube and "Like" a video.

Step 8: Navigate to the IFTTT folder in your Google Drive.

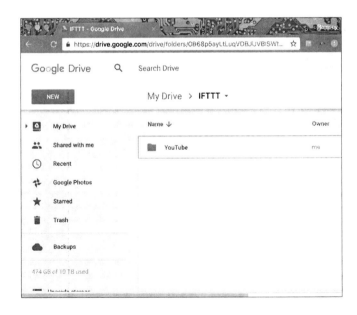

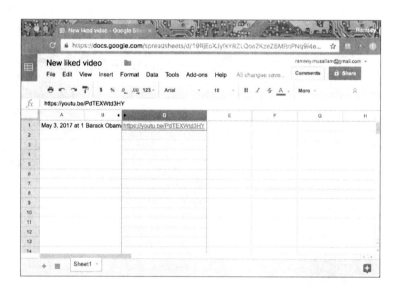

Pocket Tutorial for Saving Images

As with videos, I wanted to curate pictures that could potentially serve as Involuntary Curiosity sparks and store them in an organized, easily accessible place online. Much like YouTube, this system needed to be able to work with any web browser with the simple click of a button. To accomplish this I use an application called "Pocket" (getpocket.com). Pocket creates a recognizable button on the toolbar of any web browser and saves, tags, and organizes websites on a separate site that can be accessed from any Internet-enabled device. Much like videos stored in Google Drive, I can share my "Pocket" page with other collaborators. The screenshots below outline the process of setting up Pocket.

Step 1: Go to getpocket.com on any web browser and create an account. Once you have an account, Pocket will ask if you want to install the Pocket Extension on your web browser's toolbar. When you agree to install, the Pocket icon will appear in your toolbar.

Step 2: To save websites with media artifacts, click on the pocket icon in your browser's toolbar.

Step 3: Create a tag to organize your image artifact for a later classroom.

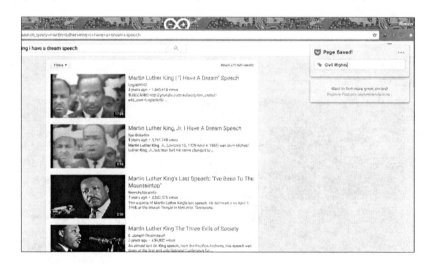

Step 4: To view the artifacts you've saved, you can go to getpocket.com or simply click on the tri-dot menu and select "Open Pocket."

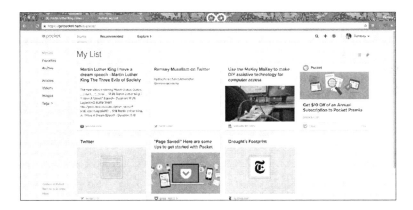

CREATE YOUR OWN CURIOSITY SPARKS

Using the earlier examples as models, use the templates below to design your own Involuntary Curiosity sparks. Remember, the goal is to find that balance between withholding and providing information in order to get students into that sweet spot on the "Curiosity vs. Confidence" chart we saw on page 15. Always try to inspire spontaneous student questioning about your topic. Once curiosity is sparked, subsequent instruction will follow naturally.

Spark #1: Missing Information

Description: Provide students with an artifact that has information strategically removed.

Goal: Spark questioning about essential elements of the topic.

1. Subject _____

2. Topic _____

3. Artifact (Link or resource)

_____

_____

4. Instructions

_____

_____

_____

_____

_____

5. Logic

_____

_____

_____

_____

6. Technology

_____

_____

Spark #2: Anticipated Solution

Description: Provide students with an artifact, usually an audio or video clip that ends early.

Goal: Spark questioning about how the clip will resolve.

1. Subject _____

2. Topic _____

3. Artifact (Link or resource)

_____

_____

_____

4. Instructions

_____

_____

_____

_____

_____

_____

_____

_____

5. Logic

_____

_____

_____

_____

6. Technology

_____

_____

Spark #3: Surprising Result

Description: Provide students with an artifact, usually an image, video clip, or reading in which the result is surprising, perplexing, or shocking.

Goal: Spark questioning in search of more details that explain the phenomena.

1. Subject _____

2. Topic _____

3. Artifact (Link or resource)

_____

_____

_____

4. Instructions

_____

_____

_____

_____

_____

_____

_____

5. Logic

_____

_____

_____

_____

6. Technology

_____

_____

SPARK SUMMARY
RULE #1: CURIOSITY COMES FIRST

- Being curious means being aware of an "information gap."

- When you have all the knowledge on a topic, you are not as curious as you could be.

- When you have no knowledge on a topic, you are not as curious as you could be.

- When a strategic amount of information is withheld, a curiosity "sweet spot" is achieved.

- Maximum curiosity yields maximum cognitive ability.

- Involuntary Curiosity is a useful tactic for classroom teachers.

- Missing information, anticipation, and surprise can spark Involuntary Curiosity.

RULE #2: EMBRACE THE MESS

Trial and error can be an important part of what we do every day in the classroom.
—*"3 RULES TO SPARK LEARNING,"* **4:30**

T WAS A TYPICAL TUESDAY EVENING during my first semester back in the classroom after surgery. Exhausted, I was covered in chalk, erasable marker, baking soda, and other random substances that had made their way onto my clothing while attempting to help high school sophomores actually learn chemistry. Walking to my car around 7 p.m. (a few hours later than I had promised my wife I would leave), I was still not sure if my lesson for the next day was "perfect" according to my new "Rules." But the drive from my classroom in San Francisco to my home in Sonoma County would take more than an hour. It was time to head home. All the way to the car, I heard the negative thoughts creeping in:

You're a freaking workaholic!

What's wrong with you?

This is why you had heart problems!

You're only a teacher!

Why are you working so hard?

What are you trying to accomplish?

It will never be perfect!

You should have used your fancy degree on a different career!

If you chose a different career you wouldn't have to drive two counties away to afford to live.

How the hell will I support my family if my lesson plans aren't perfect?

You were supposed to be a better, more efficient, "veteran" teacher after heart surgery!

I guess I'll show up an hour early tomorrow to finish planning...

I made my way out of the school's parking lot and crossed the Golden Gate Bridge, bracing for the evening Bay Area Traffic. I turned on NPR in an attempt to calm the voice in my head—the voice of the Impostor.

I heard the voice of my favorite radio show host come over the airwaves: "I'm Terry Gross, and this is *Fresh Air.*" I was excited, and then a split second later, equally discouraged. *Fresh Air* on the way home meant another late night. Another night not saying goodnight to my four children. Another night trying to explain to my wife why, even after sixteen years in the classroom and the paradigm-shifting power of a health crisis, I couldn't seem to "figure it out."

Gross continued.

"Today's guest is the host of *The Daily Show,* Jon Stewart."

A big fan of the show, and knowing it was to be Stewart's final episode that week, I turned up the volume and surrendered to the lure of Gross's calming style of entertaining interrogation. The interview began as usual with the host and guest catching up and exchanging pleasantries. Then, as if I was hit by a ton of bricks, Stewart said something that forced me to pull the car over and scribble wildly in my lesson-planning book.

Gross was grilling Stewart on his show-preparation strategies: the intricacies of the writing; the tireless review of the daily news; the rehearsal of jokes and media interludes that created the impeccable timing that made the show a work of art. None (or at least, very little) of what looked so spontaneous to the viewing audience was actually spontaneous. It required planning and attention to detail. To quote Stewart, "It is through intense structure that I find the safety to be creative."

This is something about which I had always wondered! Stewart seemed so calm on stage, so rehearsed, yet authentic, and so creative! As a teacher I couldn't help but always reflect on the work that must have gone

---

"It is through intense structure that I find the safety to be creative."

—Jon Stewart

---

into each show. Knowing the tireless effort I would put into a single lesson plan in my chemistry class, imagining Stewart's work and pressure to perform filled me with an immediate sense of anxiety. I knew an intense level of planning had to be involved in the creation of such a popular cable television show. But Stewart's ability to make a complex connection between creativity and structure in one poignant sentence rocked me like a line from a Neil Young song that carries the weight of human emotion on a few carefully curated words.

"It is through intense structure that I find the safety to be creative."

What is the structure to which Stewart is referring? In the mindset and practice of my surgeon, I had noticed a powerful pattern at work. That pattern honored the union of two seemingly different entities: structure and creativity. Creativity—often viewed as emerging from spontaneity, disorder, mess—being coupled with the word "structure" fascinated me.

With the car in park, I got out my lesson-planning book—the same book with my new Rules scribbled on the front page—and took notes as I listened.

I realized at that moment on the shoulder of Highway 101 that the exhaustion I had felt just twenty minutes prior in the parking lot was amplified by a misinterpretation of my second rule: "embrace the mess." As is evident in the previous chapter, curiosity as an instructional construct is extremely tangible. Grounded in the research literature, clear strategies can be leveraged to curate information gaps for students that can serve as windows into great instruction. Unlike curiosity, the subsequent mess of learning that would follow as my second scribbled-down Rule was less tangible.

Although my approach to teaching had completely flipped, I was still plugging along day by day, lesson by lesson. I had my three Rules in hand but possessed no overarching context to empower them and let them grow and flourish. Sparking curiosity had become my new passion. However, I saw the resulting mess of student questioning and open experimentation as something that, while meaningful, felt incredibly difficult and exhausting to manage. Curious students meant more questions to manage to which I might not know the answers, the desire to explore concepts or perform activities I might not be prepared to facilitate. These curious students created a classroom dynamic that I had no experience facilitating. In summary, I would be creating curious students with no structure to support their curiosity.

As the segment ended, I put the car back in drive and crossed the Golden Gate Bridge, all the while questioning the new approach I wanted to apply to my teaching: *It is through intense structure that I find the safety to be creative.*

I knew I had more work to do, but I also felt a sense of direction and motivation to continue to develop a context for the Rules. My thoughts shifted to other entertainers, comedians, writers, filmmakers. As a huge fan of literature and film, I had never until this moment reflected on the obvious connections between the goals of storytellers and teachers. For all intents and purposes, Jon Stewart is a storyteller. He is an artist whose goal on *The Daily Show* was to create an entertaining journey for the viewer. And, like educators, he had a specific goal in mind for his audience. Teachers may not see themselves as entertainers, but they plan lessons with the goal of creating a directed sense of meaning. The more I considered Stewart's comment, the more clear it became to me that the "structure" to which Stewart was referring was not exclusive to *The Daily Show*; it was a more universal cycle that was intrinsic to all types of storytelling.

The words of the late David Foster Wallace came to mind. Wallace was a prolific writer and literary hero of mine whose novel, *The Infinite Jest*, challenged conventional prose with its intimidating length, detailed footnotes, and simultaneous ability to captivate the reader. Wallace said this about his creative process:

"Great stories and great jokes share a lot in common. They both depend on a certain quantity of vital information removed, but evoked in such a way as to cause an explosion of associative connections within the recipient."

Wallace posits a glaring and understated connection between the engagement we feel when reading a great book, anticipating the next episode of our favorite TV series, or intensely focusing on the climax of the year's best film. As a teacher, I cannot think of anything I want more than for my students to experience "...an explosion of associative connections."

The research into curiosity reminds us that, just like the "great stories and jokes" to which Wallace alludes, all engaging tales include a mentor to whom our introduction is delayed. The mentor's arrival is in response to a gap in the story. And his wisdom provides the necessary tools to empower the story's hero, arming the hero with new information, a fresh perspective, an unlikely path, a grueling evaluation. It's in those moments that an explosion of connections occurs.

I challenge you to think of any great story, film, joke, or engaging tale where the mentor appears at the beginning. Can you imagine *Star Wars* if Yoda appeared during the first ten minutes of *The Empire Strikes Back*? Or if, in *The Karate Kid*, Mr. Miyagi took Daniel under his wing in the opening scene? Or what if in Matt Damon and Ben Affleck's heart-wrenching coming-of-age masterpiece, *Good Will Hunting*, Robin Williams' character, Sean, the sage counselor, had helped Will confront his internal struggles during the first act?

To validate the above point, one must look no further than the moment in each film mentioned above where the mentor first appears, and the context for which they are introduced to the protagonist (Figure 2.1).

Each mentor in these stories appears forty-plus minutes into the film. Their arrival is in response to a significant information gap within the hero. Luke needs to learn the Force; Daniel, self-defense; and Will, self-awareness. Despite their late arrival in the story, each teacher plays a role upon which the Hero and the story greatly depend.

I would argue that we, as teachers, often forget the importance of waiting. We feel that if only we give enough basic information upfront

When the Student is Ready, the Teacher Appears

Yoda's first appearance in *The Empire Strikes Back*: 47:15
CONTEXT: Luke Skywalker is directed by Obi-Wan Kenobi to seek guidance from Yoda in learning the ways of the Force.

Mr. Miyagi's first appearance in *The Karate Kid*: 40:56
CONTEXT: Mr. Miyagi mysteriously appears just as Daniel is being attacked by members of Cobra Kai Karate Dojo.

Sean's first appearance in *Good Will Hunting*: 41:19
CONTEXT: Sean is asked to serve as Will's therapist after a number of others tried unsuccessfully to assist him.

Figure 3.1

our students will have the tools to confront the challenges we will then present to them. While there is a lot of truth in this, we often overlook an important question: Do our students want the tools we can provide? Do they feel a need for the tools?

The practice of waiting—of delaying the mentor—does not negate or challenge the need for direct instruction. Rather it forces you to be more intentional about deciding when direct instruction is applied. This paradigm shift leverages lecture as "spackle" rather than "paint"—identifying and filling gaps in knowledge, rather than viewing students as a blank canvas.

This realization corroborated the initial success I had experienced with students in leveraging Involuntary Curiosity sparks. At the same

The practice of waiting—of delaying the mentor—forces you to be more intentional about deciding when direct instruction is applied.

time, I knew I needed a new structure that would allow me and my students to truly embrace the mess of learning. Or, as Stewart so eloquently stated, find a structure that lends the "... safety to be creative." Keeping the above stories in mind, one needs look no further than Joseph Campbell's *The Hero's Journey* to observe the prevalence of the delayed mentor in any great story's architecture.

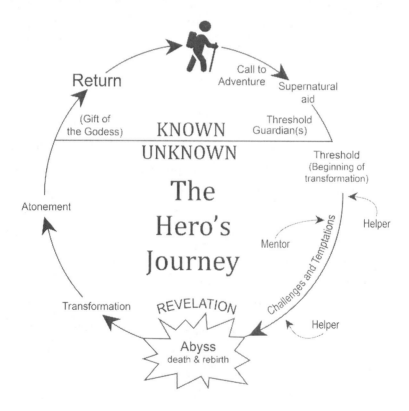

When I look thoughtfully at the diagram above, I am once again reminded of my surgeon. His "Call to Adventure" included negotiating the challenging particulars associated with complex open-heart surgery. The "Mentors" were those who served as his collaborators and teachers along the way. He experienced "Challenges" as he acquired and developed new skills. Finally, his "Transformation" occurred when he successfully performed the operation and emerged as a professional armed with a newly mastered procedure. When I look even closer, I see the three rules upon which this book is founded: Curiosity. Mess. Reflection. I see a context that leverages the mess and creates a structure for the second Rule.

What if we viewed *students* as heroes and our lesson plans as their journey? Why not!? It works in Hollywood, at publishing houses, and on Comedy Central. Why not in the classroom? Why can't "stoichiometry" be viewed with the same vigor as Odysseus's return from the Trojan War? Albeit corny, I would argue that the similarities between modern, branded learning cycles embraced by schools of education and *The Hero's Journey* are not just a strange coincidence.

This "coincidence" is vividly clear when positioning the 5E Learning Cycle, a common format embraced by many schools of education, along the generic diagram of the Hero's Journey. It makes complete sense that the universal sequence of events that drives any hero toward mastery and transformation are universal constructs that should be present in any inquiry-learning cycle designed to facilitate student application of content and academic transformation. The table and diagram on the next page outline the striking parallels between the structure of the Hero's Journey and the structure of the 5E Learning Cycle.

The Hero's Journey		The 5E Learning Cycle
The Call to Adventure	←→	Engage
The Challenge	←→	Explore
The Mentor	←→	Explain
The Transformation	←→	Extend
The Return	←→	Evaluate

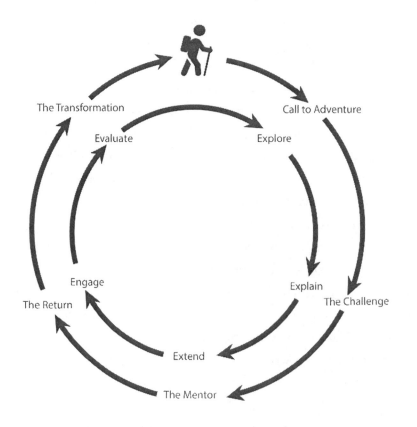

Using a structure that combines the Hero's Journey and the 5E Learning Cycle, I created a new lesson-planning template. This template serves as a strong reminder that I am "crafting" rather than writing lesson plans. Disorder and mess will happen, but they occur in the context of a journey that I have curated for my students to propel forward momentum. And that entire journey grounds the initial curiosity spark in a meaningful context: Embrace the mess by embracing "intense structure to find the safety to be creative." The purpose of the template is not to simply facilitate a learning cycle, rather it is to spark a journey of curiosity and discovery that leads to an explosion of meaningful learning connections.

In the template that follows, "Phase 1: The Call to Adventure," or in 5E language, "Engage," would embody the Involuntary Curiosity spark discussed in the previous chapter. It is designed to be a structure to help you provide context for the Involuntary Curiosity spark—or according to the Hero's Journey parallel, the "Call to Adventure." I have absolutely fallen in love with lesson planning this way. I never tell my students that I am indeed thinking of each cycle of learning as a Hero's Journey, but planning in such a way is so exciting for me. This template provides the *intense structure* I was looking for to be truly creative in the classroom and to embrace the mess in a directed way. Long gone are the days of planning day by day and lesson by lesson. Now, I plan lessons with a long-range view, and let the details and the mess sit beneath a strong pedagogical framework.

Hero's Journey/5E Learning Cycle Example

Subject—Physics

Topic—Circuits

Phase 1: Call to Adventure/ENGAGE—An artifact is presented to spark student involuntary curiosity about the topic. (See page 18 for more info.)

Instructions

Display the *Squishy Circuits* image showing two LED bulbs wired in series. After showing students the image, ask them to recreate the image using the materials provided (cup of Play-Doh, 9V battery with leads, two LEDs).

Desired Questions

- How many bulbs can you light at once?
- Are the red and black wires different?
- Is the energy from the battery going through the Play-Doh?

Phase 2: Challenge/EXPLORE—A challenge task that forces students to answer their own questions and/or surfaces an awareness in the student that more information is needed to complete the task.

Instructions

- Give students three more LEDs. Now that students have found success lighting two bulbs, challenge students to light five bulbs simultaneously without the bulbs dimming.

Note: Because the initial image shows two bulbs lit, the goal is to tempt students to light all five bulbs in the same format. Five bulbs will not light this way, and thus, students will have to invent a new way to light the bulbs. Ultimately some students will discover that the bulbs must be branched off of the Play-Doh rather than aligned in single file. In doing so, students either develop an awareness of the need for new information, or invent new information that they will learn later in the learning cycle (series-versus-parallel circuitry). See images below.

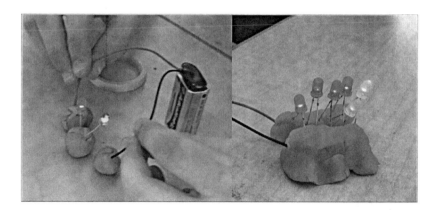

Phase 3: Meeting the Mentor/EXPLAIN—A tailored lecture is presented where necessary information and tools are shared with students.

Instructions

- Show the below images to students and relate each image conceptually to its respective *Squishy Circuits* counterpart invented in Phase 2. "Spackle" in necessary content such as vocabulary (series-versus-parallel circuitry), equations (calculating series-versus-parallel resistance).

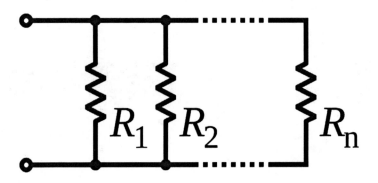

Note: If you are planning on implementing this lesson and do not have a solid background in physics, a nice explanation of content can be found here: khanacademy.org/science/physics/circuits-topic.

Phase 4: Transformation/EXTEND—A new challenge task is presented which requires students to extend knowledge of the topic.

Instructions

- Given the materials provided (9V battery and battery leaders, string of Christmas tree lights, wire cutters, hot glue, and cardboard), build an "Electric House" from cardboard or foam board that contains both series and parallel circuitry. Draw and label a proper circuit diagram for your house.

Phase 5: Return/EVALUATE—A public product is created to demonstrate knowledge and growth in the topic.

Instructions

- Assign students the task of creating and publishing an *Instructable* (instructables.com) that outlines the conceptual and quantitative process for designing and calculating the resistance in their electric house. (See page 121 for more info about leveraging *Instructables* as an assessment tool.)

CREATE YOUR OWN HERO'S JOURNEY/5E LEARNING CYCLE

Subject _____

Topic _____

Phase 1: Call to Adventure/ENGAGE—An artifact is presented to spark student involuntary curiosity about the topic.

Instructions

_____

_____

_____

_____

_____

_____

Desired Questions

Phase 2: Challenge/EXPLORE—A challenge task that forces students to answer their own questions and/or surfaces an awareness in the student that more information is needed to complete the task.

Instructions

Phase 3: Meeting the Mentor/EXPLAIN—A tailored lecture is presented where necessary information and tools are shared with students.

Instructions

_____

_____

_____

_____

_____

Phase 4: Transformation/EXTEND—A new challenge task is presented which requires students to extend knowledge of the topic.

Instructions

_____

_____

_____

_____

_____

Phase 5: Return/EVALUATE—A public product is created to demonstrate knowledge and growth in the topic.

Instructions

_____

_____

_____

_____

_____

HERO'S JOURNEY INSTRUCTIONAL CHECKLIST

Upon crafting a learning cycle according to the above template, I always assess my lesson against the checklist shown below. Consider it lesson plan "quality control."

- Was a situation presented to spark authentic student questioning about the topic first?
- Were students challenged to provide explanations to their question(s)?
- Was lecture used as "spackle" rather than "paint"?
- Were students asked to visibly master specific skills, techniques, and processes in class?
- Were students challenged to extend content to new and more complex scenarios?
- Were students required to produce a public product to demonstrate understanding?

Using Technology for Additional Structure and Organization

With respect to technology, given the more amorphous construct of "mess" versus the tangible tutorials associated with sparking Involuntary Curiosity, specific technology-integration strategies are harder to identify. Despite this difficulty, I have found the use of simple Google Doc templates where students track their progress through a learning cycle to be extremely helpful for both teacher and student.

By replacing /edit at the end of any public Google document's address with /copy, you can create a template that can easily be pushed out to each student's individual Google Drive. The student can then share that Google Doc with the teacher, who can monitor the student's progress through the entire learning cycle. This simple hack removes the extra step of asking students to "Make a copy" of a Google Doc, or the need for more advanced scripts or programs that automate the process.

Tip: Replace /edit at the end of any public Google document's address with /copy to create a template for others to use.

Google Doc Template Tutorial

The screenshots below outline the process of setting up the Google Doc template I use for each learning cycle.

Step 1: Create a Google Doc.

Step 2: Edit the document to include what you would like the students to record.

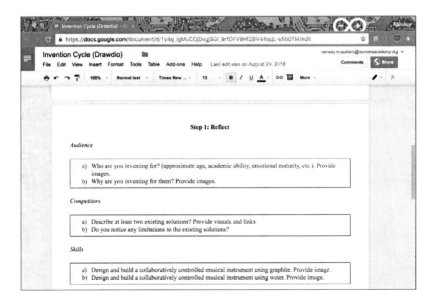

Step 3: Click on the Share button to change the link-sharing settings to "Public on the web" and "Can view."

Step 4: Change address of the file ending from /edit to /copy.

Step 5: Share address and instruct students to "Make a copy."

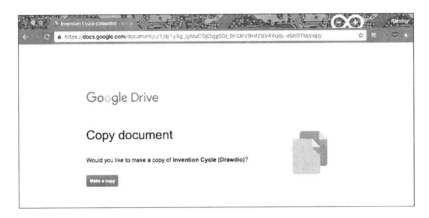

CURIOSITY SPARKED?
Here's a space to jot down your ideas.

SPARK SUMMARY
RULE #2: EMBRACE THE MESS

- Learning is destined to become "messy" when a curriculum is guided by student curiosity.

- A structure that organizes and leverages the inevitable mess empowers greater learning opportunities.

- Joseph Campbell's *The Hero's Journey* provides an authentic and common sense structure.

- The phases of the 5E Learning Cycle align perfectly with the phases of the Hero's Journey.

RULE #3: PRACTICE REFLECTION

What we do is important. It deserves our care. It also deserves our revision.

—"3 RULES TO SPARK LEARNING," 4:42

EFLECTION. What a tired, overused word this has become in education circles. Common sense tells us it is essential, even mandatory, for growth. How does anyone, teacher or student, evolve and grow without reflecting—embracing victories and learning from mistakes—and adjusting lessons accordingly? Reflection is an obvious necessity in the practice of being an effective teacher or student.

For my surgeon, the commitment to reflecting on personal practice and learning continually from the practice of others (through both conversation and the reading of journal publications), literally meant the difference between life and death. Likewise, the structures and resources we as educators take advantage of to grow and evolve can also mean the difference between a banal or transformative life after school. However, unlike the learned, metacognitive behavior embodied by my surgeon, practicing reflection continues to be very challenging for me.

I have come to realize that the tangible difference between the type of reflection my surgeon discussed and the type we toss around in blogs, at conferences, and on faculty in-service days is the perceived notion of "high stakes." Unlike the moment when my surgeon literally held my life in his hands as he made delicate stitches in my aorta, the impact we make on our students is often not felt until years after graduation day.

Described by a former colleague as the "ultimate act of faith," the invisible string that connects our lesson plans to our students' lives years down the line can create a false sense of security in our craft. Because the immediate effects of our instruction are not visible, growing satisfied, perhaps even complacent, is all too common in the teaching community. Rather than spurring us to digging into journals, this false sense of security tricks us into creating a binder of lesson plans to reuse each year. Instead, we should be scratching successful lessons in order to take a risk with new ideas and observing colleagues so we can learn from others' ideas—and steal the best ones. We should be writing it all down, noting everything, and authentically incorporating what we learn. We should think of our classrooms as operating rooms: delicate, yet powerful, places where transformation can occur. After all, as students ourselves, we are (or should be) growing and changing until our last day.

I remember calling my mother after the end of my first chemistry class on my first day of teaching. Indescribably exhausted, I boasted that

I had made it through the class. She comforted me with a phrase I'm sure all new teachers have sought refuge in: "I know it feels hard now, but when you gain more experience, you will be able to use your lesson plans year after year." It was an innocent, loving comment that drastically over-simplified the complexity associated with growing as an educator. Indeed, it is part truth and part trap.

So how do we do as the surgeon does with a vulnerable patient on the operating table and continue to improve? Much like the strategies for sparking Involuntary Curiosity and the framework of the Hero's Journey/5E Learning Cycle, proper reflection demands a dependable, consistent template that can guide us well beyond the conference, in-service meet, or the myriad of posts in the education blogosphere.

As shared in this book's introductory chapter, my introduction to the world of genuine, honest, reflective practice was emotionally challenging to say the least. My inner voice shouted, *Impostor!* Perhaps you've heard the same voice while reading anonymous student feedback, or insecurely trolling ratemyteacher.com, or when interacting with a more "popular"

We must strive to be consistent and brand the process of reflection as expected and necessary, rather than shocking and feared.

---

colleague, or struggling to create a good lesson plan. When that voice sneaks in, it's difficult to hear beyond it, which is why I believe reflection must be structured in a way that mirrors behaviors that do not carry so much emotional baggage. We must strive to be consistent and brand the process of reflection as expected and necessary, rather than shocking and feared.

In the months and years scribbling my new pedagogical approach on that front page of my lesson-planning book, I have designed a format for practicing reflection that has propelled me into more authentic and effective teaching. Before I discuss specific methods and associated strategies, it is important to note three behaviors that must be present if reflection is to be truly transformative.

Effective reflection must . . .

Be consistent—incorporated into our daily lesson planning routine.

Be honest—empowered by authentic, objective, and blunt feedback.

Be mutual—done by students and teachers.

Keeping these three behaviors in mind, the following suggested strategies for reflection are very simple, perhaps overly simple. However, the brevity of each has made all the difference in creating a consistent, honest, and mutual system for reflection that is sustainable.

In addition to the strategies, I've included associated technology tutorials when applicable. I have divided the strategies into techniques to help organize and empower teacher reflection as well as techniques to help organize and empower student reflection.

REFLECTION TECHNIQUES FOR TEACHERS

1. Email to Blog Post

Overview

Publicly reflecting on a blog after each class forces me to confront what worked and what didn't. It also connects me with colleagues outside of my school. Despite its importance, sharing my work on a daily basis can feel like an arduous task after a long school day. By using Blogger's

"Post using email" feature, I can quickly publish a blog by simply sending an email. Because emailing is integrated seamlessly into all smartphone devices, this strategy allows me to quickly reflect while walking to my car, riding the bus, or having a cup of coffee. (See all of my blog reflections at: cyclesoflearning.com/learning--instruction.)

Technology

- Computer
- Smartphone or Tablet
- Blogger App (accessible through drive.google.com)

Tutorial

Step 1: Visit "Blogger" and create a "New Blog."

Step 2: Navigate to "Settings" and click "Email."

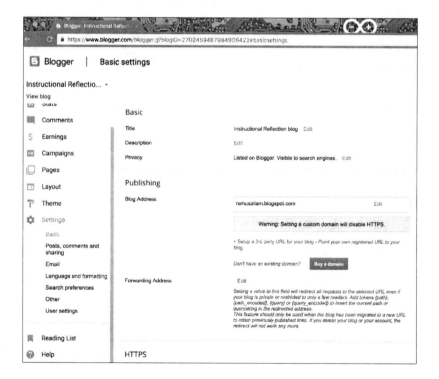

Step 3: Under "Posting using email" add a "secret word" to create a private email address. When you send an email to this address, the subject line will become the blog title, and the text included in the email will become the text body of the blog post. Any pictures or video attached to the email will embed in the blog.

Step 4: Compose and send an email to the address you chose. By saving this address as a contact in your smartphone, you can quickly send the email and seamlessly post to your blog.

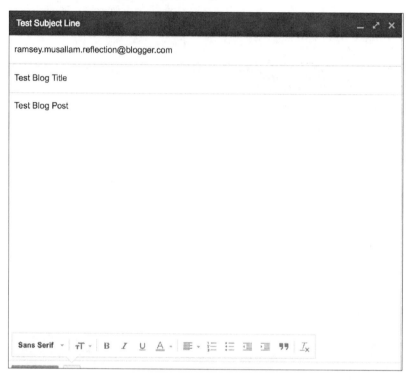

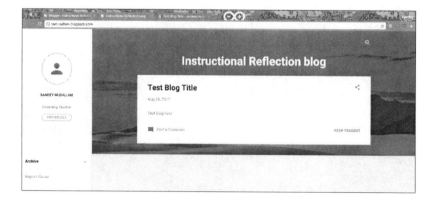

2. Double Lesson Planning

Overview

Never am I more aware of what worked and failed in a lesson plan than the moments directly after my students walk out of the classroom. I'm left with an incredible rush that occurs when things go exactly to plan—or a soul-sinking feeling if the lesson plan was a complete bomb. To leverage the clarity those few moments provide, I created a lesson-planning outline in a Google Doc table that has one column for this year and another column for next year. Simply noting what I will change in a different color adds a level of relief and saves my thoughts on revisions in a common place for reflection and comparison.

Technology

- Computer
- Smartphone or Tablet
- Google Drive (drive.google.com)

Tutorial

Step 1: Create a Google Doc.

Step 2: Create a table with a column for "Lesson Plans (this year)" and "Lesson Plans (next year)." Add plenty of rows, one for each lesson-plan outline for a specific day.

Step 3: Create an outline for the day's lesson in the left column. I typically note where I am in the Hero's Journey 5E Learning Cycle (see page 62) and then create a detailed plan including links and images needed, etc., on our class website later. Despite the brevity of this first step, planning in a table helps me organize my ideas prior to gathering resources and helps me view my lesson-planning cycle "chunks" rather than the day-to-day grind. It also sets up a nice structure for sustainable and meaningful reflection. I've even shared this document with my students to emphasize the importance of the reflection process in everything we do.

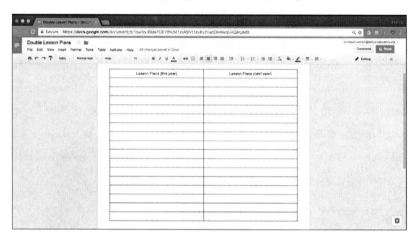

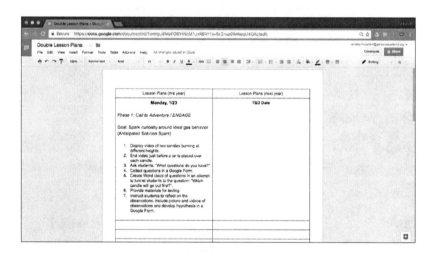

Step 4: Immediately after students leave the room, copy and paste the outline to the "Lesson Plan (next year)" column on the right. Note your desired revisions in red text. When planning my lessons next year, this column will become the column on the left, and I will pay close attention to things noted in red as adjustments to make.

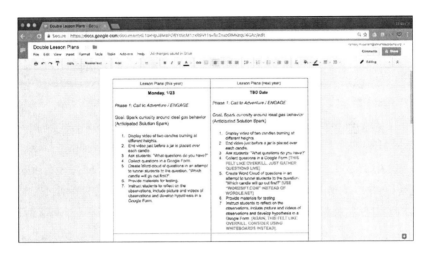

3. Mobile "Prep" Desk

Overview

During the past sixteen years, I have experimented with many different methods for using my prep period. Last school year I shared my classroom with a colleague who taught English during my prep period. My colleague said it was fine if I stayed in the room to plan lessons during his class, and what began as a simple way to save time turned into a transformative experience. Throughout the course of the year, I observed more than 100 English lessons, watching the art of teaching occur from a completely different angle and content domain. As the year progressed, I sensed my own teaching—and, more importantly, awareness of what good teaching looks like—shift and transform, assuming a more diverse definition. Best of all, this accidental system for reflection fit perfectly into my own busy schedule as I was able to complete my lesson plans as well.

I decided to continue with this efficient and informal method of learning from my colleagues this school year (2015-2016). At the beginning of the school year I asked four different teachers—from four different disciplines—if I could spend my prep period in their classrooms. Each quarter, I would switch classes. I'm in the middle of this process right now, having spent the first quarter in the classroom of an algebra teacher and the second in the classroom of a theatre teacher. The next two quarters will be spent in a computer science and fellow chemistry teachers' classroom.

I cannot overemphasize how incredibly impactful and simple this process has been. Each day I leave my prep period with my lessons planned and an invaluable list of strategies I want to try. I also have a greater awareness of what students experience as they move from class to class.

I encourage you to spend your prep period in the classroom of another teacher. Here's some food for thought: What if schools required that teacher prep periods were stationed in the back of another teacher's classroom? What if those stations changed each quarter? Peer-to-peer learning and solidarity would occur naturally and would be ingrained in the culture of the school rather than being forced awkwardly as a system of infrequent classroom "walk-throughs" or observations done simply to complete required paperwork.

What if peer-to-peer learning and solidarity occurred naturally and were ingrained in your school's culture?

Student Reflection Techniques

1. Three Thoughtful Questions

Overview

As should be expected, traditional summative assessments such as individual examinations, quizzes, and in-class essays can be stressful experiences for students. Moreover, while some students move smoothly right through the exam, many others constantly bombard their teachers with questions to which they know the answer or—with some thought—could figure out. From my experience, the tendency to ask too many questions can often be a symptom of test-taking anxiety rather than a lack of preparation. While I am sympathetic to this situation, I always struggle with answering too many questions, as I feel my responses do more to enable and feed their stress rather than empower their ability to navigate complex situations.

Last year I experimented with a system called "Three Thoughtful Questions" that has completely altered the way students ask questions during an individual assessment. This system has introduced a level of student self-reflection that has transformed the test-taking environment in my classroom. The process is incredibly simple! At the top of each assessment, I print three question marks. Students are allowed to ask any clarifying question they want during the assessment. Each time they ask a question, I cross off a question mark until all are gone. When all question marks are crossed off, they can no longer ask any questions. Such a simple system has drastically improved my students' ability to think critically about their questions, subconsciously categorizing them into high and low importance. It has transformed what used to be a stressful situation for students into one filled with critical thought. The quality of student questioning has improved, and more importantly, their metacognitive skills have grown dramatically! It works for timeouts in football. Why not in the classroom?

2. Daily Journal Form

Overview

I have experimented with numerous methods for promoting student reflection after a lesson: Exit Ticket Questions, Silent Journaling, and High Point/Low Point to name a few. While effective from time to time, none truly gave me a chance to collect meaningful student reflection while simultaneously implementing a system of student accountability. With new updates to Google Forms that allow students to upload attachments, such as images and videos, student reflections that include media artifacts as evidence of learning are simple to acquire. Text reflections and uploaded artifacts are saved to the same Google Sheet, simplifying the review process and archiving reflections in an organized way for future reference.

Technology

- Computer, Smartphone, or Tablet
- Google Drive (drive.google.com)

Tutorials

Step 1: Create a new Google Form.

Step 2: Create a question with a "Paragraph" response field and click on the "File upload" option.

Step 3: Instruct students to complete their reflections and add a media artifact of learning.

Step 4: Access Google Sheet with responses and analyze student reflections.

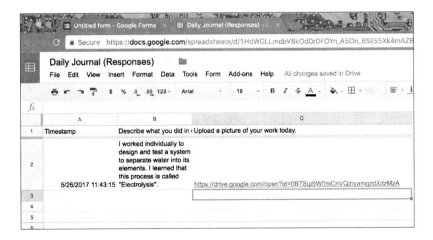

3. Homework Blog Reflections

Overview

The "No Homework" movement is extremely popular in many education circles. While philosophically I do agree with limiting homework's importance as an assessment device, I feel strongly that the teacher, as the artist of the learning cycle, can create meaningful ways to leverage student work outside of the regular schedule as an effective pedagogical tool. To this end, a few years ago I designed a homework system that not only empowers students as developing digital citizens but also instills a culture of deep reflection.

In the past, I would assign homework problems (e.g., Chapter 2, 1–10, etc.) and check them off casually the next day in class. While this process fed my gradebook with consistent numbers, I never really knew if students invested in the problems, or frantically copied the problem down prior to entering class. Rather than continue with this at-times arduous process, I decided to leverage my students' online presence in an additional way. Today, all of my students maintain a blog portfolio where they provide a review, including images and videos, of their work over the course of a topic of study.

Rather than not assigning homework problems, I decided to quit grading homework in class. Instead, I asked students to keep track of the problems they did not understand. When it came time for them to produce their blog posts at the conclusion of a particular topic of study, I asked students to reflect publicly on their struggles, questions, and realizations when doing their homework. Not only has this system increased student awareness of their own knowledge, but the public forum for reflection has notably amplified student motivation and accountability around completing homework. Additionally, it has contributed to decreased student stress when they do not understand a particular assignment because it offers an environment where students strive naturally for deeper understanding. The screenshot below is from a student's reflection on homework assigned during a topic of study in chemistry.

Technology

- Computer, Smartphone, or Tablet
- Blogger (blogger.com)

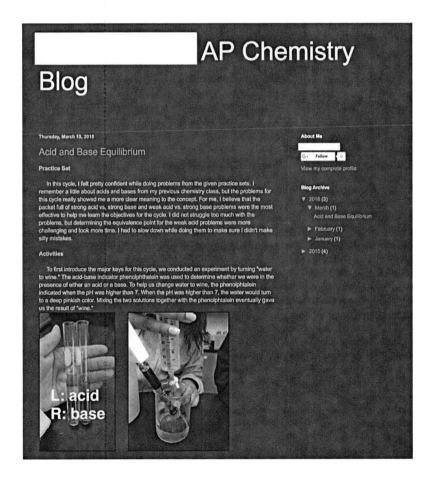

SPARK SUMMARY
RULE #3: PRACTICE REFLECTION

- Reflection is best when it is consistent, honest, and mutual.

- Blogging, reflective lesson planning, and peer observation are powerful teacher strategies.

- Exam question strategies, journals, and homework reflections are powerful student strategies.

- Google Drive and Blogger are examples of technology partners.

CONCLUSION

But if we as educators leave behind this simple role as disseminators of content and embrace a new paradigm as cultivators of curiosity and inquiry, we just might bring a little bit more meaning to their school day—and spark their imagination.

—*"3 RULES TO SPARK LEARNING," 5:59*

CURIOSITY, DISORDER, AND REFLECTION. These are the three constructs that reframed the way I see my vocation as a teacher. They emerged through personal trauma and now provide a powerful lens to sharpen each lesson plan I create. I am hopeful that this book has helped you reflect on ways you can inspire authentic student inquiry, embrace the necessary, inevitable mess of learning, and discover new ways to reflect and adjust your teaching in response to your students. It's hard to believe that after sixteen years in the classroom and six years of graduate school, these three constructs have proven to be the most powerful instructional tools I have encountered—more powerful than any "edu" buzzwords or acronyms I have come across.

It might come as no surprise that a book designed to help teachers spark authentic learning cycles places curiosity as its first tenant. Central to cultivating curiosity is the curation (or revealing) of an information gap, followed by a gradual release of information, strategically withholding just enough to create the desire for more. A delayed mentor (you!) comes in with a responsive approach to direct instruction that leverages a lecture as education "spackle" rather than "paint."

Leveraging disorder and practicing reflection are extensions of a curiosity-first curriculum.

I would argue that leveraging disorder and practicing reflection are extensions of a curiosity-first curriculum. When student questions are placed before teacher voice, learning in the classroom mirrors learning everywhere else in our world. The teacher is an information "gap filler," a coach who knows when—and when not—to lend a helping hand. Rather than being the guru, the teacher is a cultivator of inquiry and a quencher of curiosity. Lecture is no longer seen as a "bad word" in education, but instead, viewed as a powerful tool to be used in the context of the Hero's Journey that has been carefully orchestrated. What an incredibly meaningful way to view our vocation!

Sprinkled throughout this book are technology integration tutorials that I have found to be helpful in streamlining, organizing, and empowering the rules I have shared. Those tools, although simple and possessing broad applications, are implemented through an intentional pedagogical strategy. This approach allows me to view technology as a strategic partner, freeing me from the need to use all the tools and from the guilt of not being as "innovative" as I need to be.

Teaching is an incredibly personal and public endeavor requiring our energy, creativity, and deep authenticity. In the words of the educator Parker Palmer, "Good teaching cannot be reduced to technique. Good teaching comes from the identity and integrity of the teacher."

Whether the perspective shared in this book resonated with you, or you have developed your own structure that works for your students, I encourage you to view technology and other external tools as just that: tools. Each time I wander through a vendor hall at a conference, I ask myself the same question: Does the tool in front of me help empower my three rules? If the answer is yes, I will give it a try. If not, I move on.

I challenge you to develop your own overarching structure, mission statement, or manifesto. Let it serve as a guide that empowers your lesson plans and guides you through the myriad of options that can, at times, seem too overwhelming to handle.

I once heard a colleague say: "Plan in the 80s; revise for today!" I love this concept! It reminds me that great teaching has always happened (and will always happen) separately from current fads or movements in education that are external to authentic student learning. Although tools may change, I am hopeful that the three rules I scribbled down in my lesson-planning notebook will never need to be erased. With a curious mind, an appreciation for trial and error, and the confidence to be a reflective practitioner, my intention and fervent hope is that I will continue to grow as an educator until my last day in the classroom. I hope the same for you!

10 BONUS STRATEGIES

Flipping a boring lecture from the classroom to the screen of a mobile device might save instructional time, but if it is the focus of our students' experience, it's the same dehumanizing chatter just wrapped up in fancy clothing.

—*"3 RULES TO SPARK LEARNING," 1:48*

T HE MISSION OF THIS BOOK was to share with you three "rules" around which I structure my teaching, but like all educators I lean on many different strategies to help my students along on their Hero's Journey. Outlined below are ten curated techniques that do not fit neatly within this book's framework, but I leverage on a consistent basis to engage, assess, or challenge my students.

I chose to share these strategies, not because they are comprehensive, intricate, sit at the top of the Bloom's Taxonomy Pyramid, or have been rigorously tested for their efficacy. I chose them because, during the past sixteen years in the classroom, I keep coming back to them, year after year. They always seem to surface at that Critical Moment when a lesson goes from mediocre to good—or from good to great.

1. The Mistake Game

Overview

Rather than simply solving a particular problem or responding to a certain prompt, students are challenged to provide an answer while embedding one subtle mistake in their solution for their classmates to catch. To catch the mistakes created by their classmates, students must be able to solve a particular problem correctly, but more importantly, must understand the intricacies of the problem on a deep and specific level.

Technology

- Computer
- Google Drive (drive.google.com)

Tutorial

Step 1: Create a Google Slides Presentation

Step 2: Insert questions in the "Click to add notes" section.

Step 3: Distribute question slides to groups of students with sharing set to "Public on web" and "Can edit."

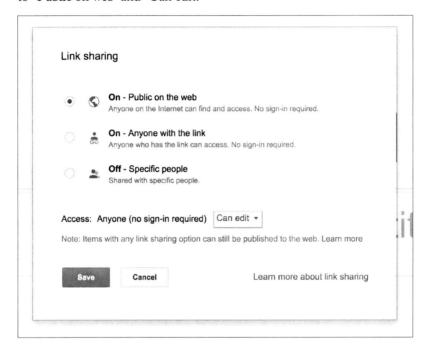

Step 4: Instruct groups to write the solution to their problems—with a mistake embedded—on a piece of white paper using a black sharpie pen. When they are done, ask them to use their computer's webcam to take a picture of their paper and insert the image directly into the appropriate slide using Google Slides' "Take a Snapshot" feature.

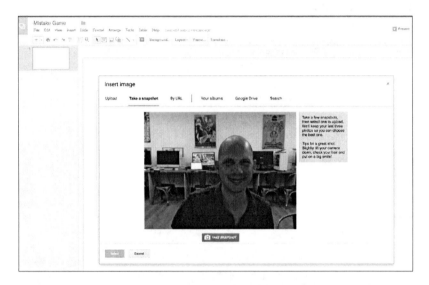

Step 5: Have students review one another's slides and try to catch and correct mistakes.

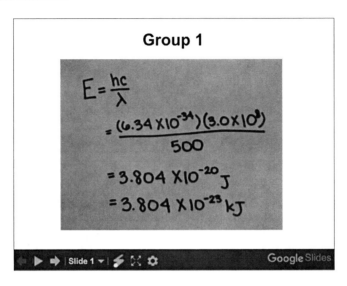

2. Group Text Message Challenges

Overview

Using the group text messaging application, "Remind," surprise students during lunch or break with a challenge question texted directly to their smartphone; for example, *First person to come to my classroom and... gets...* Because the majority of older students communicate via text, this application meets them where they are. This method has really worked in getting students' attention and engaging them in the learning process.

Technology

- Computer, Smartphone, or Tablet
- Remind (remind.com)

Tutorial

Step 1: Make a "Remind" account, create a class, and add students.

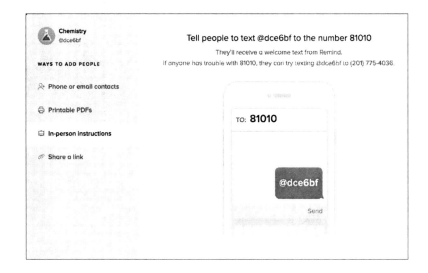

Step 2: Create a text message by clicking on "Class announcement."

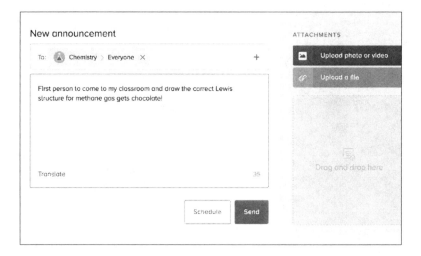

Step 3: Send your text message and wait for your students to respond.

3. Lower Blooms Basketball

Overview

Regardless of the subject area, there are times when students must assimilate procedural content. Whether it is conjugating verbs, manipulating variables, or diagramming a sentence, assimilating content considered to be "Lower Bloom's" (algorithmic, procedural, mechanical, etc.) is a small but essential step in the Hero's Journey. Using strips of paper that contain Lower Bloom's problems, have students write down the answer, crumple up the paper into "basketballs," and shoot them into a classroom "hoop."

Tutorial

Step 1: Create short problems on paper and cut into strips.

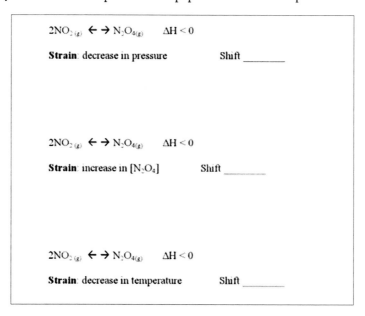

Step 2: Set up a "hoop."

Step 3: Instruct students to solve a problem, crumple it up, and take a shot. Repeat process.

4. Flipping Multiple Choice

Overview

It is a guarantee that our students will be given a multiple-choice assessment during their academic journey. Rather than being a nuisance, multiple-choice questions can be an exciting opportunity to develop higher-order thinking. A powerful twist to the multiple-choice question is to remove the question stem, presenting only the answer. Students are then challenged to create their own question stems that interact best with the observed choices.

Technology

- Computer, Smartphone, or Tablet
- Google Drive (drive.google.com)
- Screenshot

    Mac: Command + Shift + 4
    PC: "Print Screen"
    iOS Device: Home + Sleep/Wake Buttons (simultaneously)
    Android Device: Volume + Power Buttons (simultaneously)

- Image Annotation

Tutorial

Step 1: Find a screenshot of an appropriate multiple-choice question. Conceptual questions are best.

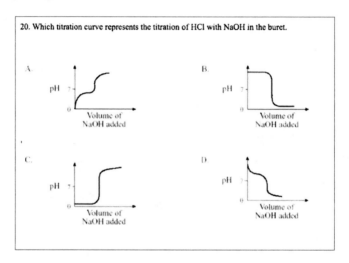

Step 2: Remove the question by adding a box over the question using your favorite image annotation technique.

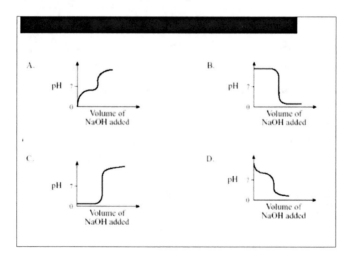

Step 3: Create a Google Form and challenge students to create their own question and share with the class. When sharing is complete, reveal the actual question.

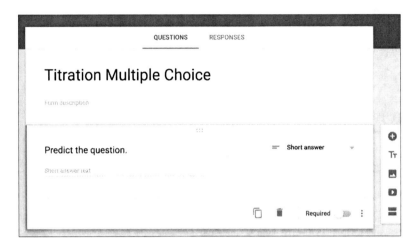

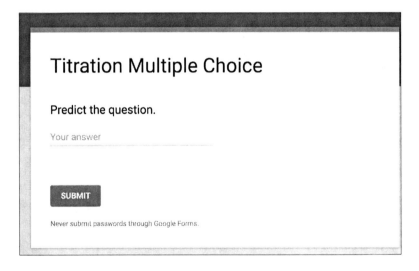

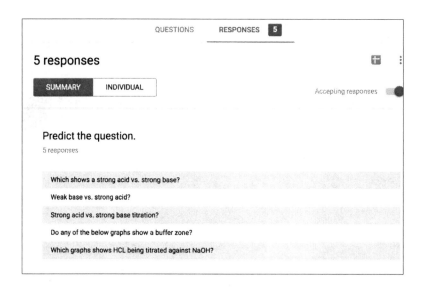

5. LEVERAGING THE "CONFIRMATION MESSAGE"

Overview

A Google Form is a powerful way to obtain student information. That being said, when using a Google Form as an assessment device, it is beneficial to provide students with feedback after they submit the form. By placing solutions in the "confirmation message" text, students receive feedback tailored to the time they submit. Additionally, because you can see multiple submissions, it is easy to see if students have submitted a junk answer to receive the solution.

Technology

- Computer, Smartphone, or Tablet
- Google Drive (drive.google.com)

Tutorial

Step 1: Create a Google Form.

Step 2: Add questions to the Google Form.

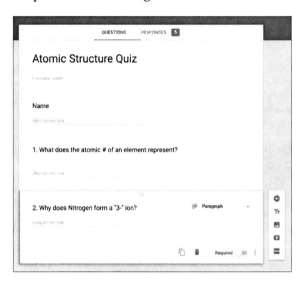

Step 3: Add solutions to "Confirmation Message."

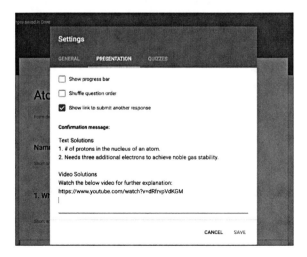

Atomic Structure Quiz

Name

Your answer

1. What does the atomic # of an element represent?

Your answer

2. Why does Nitrogen form a "3-" ion?

Your answer

SUBMIT

Step 4: Share with students. Once the Form is submitted, solutions will be displayed.

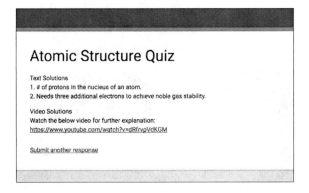

Atomic Structure Quiz

Text Solutions
1. # of protons in the nucleus of an atom.
2. Needs three additional electrons to achieve noble gas stability.

Video Solutions
Watch the below video for further explanation:
https://www.youtube.com/watch?v=dRfrvpVdKGM

Submit another response

6. Review Game Buzzer

Overview

Although different systems exist for assessment-review games (e.g., socrative.com, kahoot.it), Google Forms are a simple, efficient, and device-agnostic method for collecting spontaneous student responses. Create a Form with space for recording multiple-choice and text answers. Student responses are time stamped and saved in a spreadsheet that the teacher can monitor, take notes in, and share back to students.

Technology

- Computer, Smartphone, or Tablet
- Google Drive (drive.google.com)

Tutorials

Step 1: Create a Google Form.

Step 2: Add the multiple-choice question. Be sure to include an "Other" option to allow for text responses as well.

Step 3: Observe results. A time stamp will indicate who submitted their answers first if the game is timed.

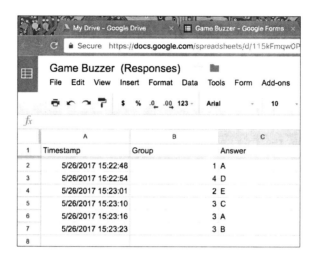

7. Virtual Office Hours

Online review sessions with students can be challenging. While Google Hangouts (hangouts.google.com) and other systems such as Skype (skype.com) and GoToMeeting (gotomeeting.com) can be effective, size limits and technology firewalls get in the way. A public Google Doc with question and answer columns is a simple solution that provides a forum for students to ask questions. The document can be revisited later for review and reflection.

Technology

- Computer, Smartphone, or Tablet
- Google Drive (drive.google.com)

Tutorials

Step 1: Create a Google Doc.

Step 2: Distribute the document link to students with sharing set to "Public on web" and "Can edit."

Step 3: Create a table with two columns, one titled "Question" and the other titled "Answer." Add at least 100 rows to leave ample space for student questions.

Step 4: Answer questions as they come in. I set a time frame (6 p.m.–9 p.m.) on a specific day when students can ask questions prior to a major assessment or project. I then select a few students to assist me in answering the questions that evening.

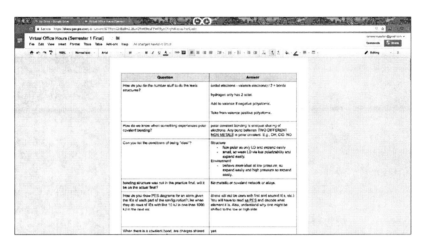

8. Instructables!

I firmly believe in the value of displaying student work publicly. This year (2017) I experimented with having students produce "Instructables" (an online "how-to" site). Students can create an Instructable for anything they have created—from a great story to a complex robotic device. Because the Instructable site is highly used by students and adults, with a larger international community, I found that students were much more motivated than when creating online instructional videos, blogs, or websites.

Technology

- Computer, Smartphone, or Tablet
- Instructables (instructables.com)

Tutorials

Step 1: Instruct students to create an "Instructables" account.

Step 2: Have students create a "New Instructable" following the on-screen instructions. When they complete the Instructable, have them share the final link with you.

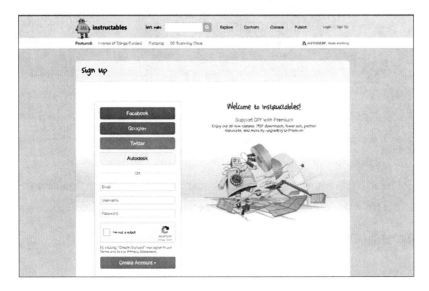

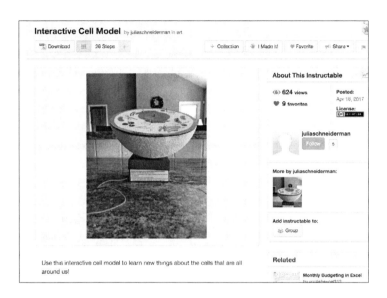

9. Student-Created Curiosity Sparks

As discussed in the first rule, Curiosity Comes First, I begin every topic by trying to withhold the perfect amount of information. (See page 17.) The goal is to motivate and, for a lack of a better word, "manipulate" students into asking a question. After a few months of this process, prior to beginning a new unit, I give groups of students targeted questions and challenge them to create an artifact (picture or video clip) that sparks their peers' curiosity and entices them to ask questions.

10. Extrapolating from Word Clouds

As discussed on page 24, Word Cloud is a type of data visualization where the size of each word indicates its frequency of use. Whenever I am confronted with something to teach that involves a list, categories, rules, etc., for which students have prior knowledge (e.g., "What are the signs of a chemical reaction?"), gathering student ideas in a Google Form, then copying responses into a Word Cloud generator, often creates a visualization that, if analyzed well, contains an organization we are looking for.

Technology

- Computer, Phone, or Tablet
- Google Drive (drive.google.com)
- Word Sift (wordsift.com)

Tutorials

Step 1: Create a Google Form with questions in order to gather student responses.

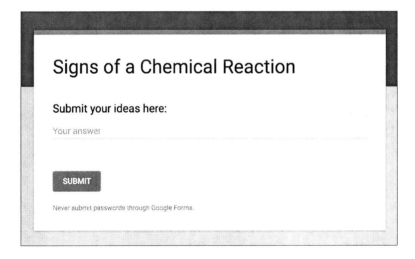

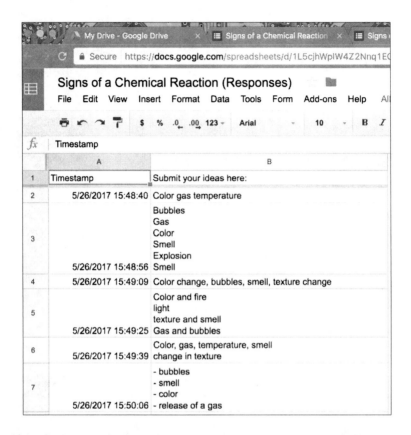

Step 2: Copy student responses into "Word Sift" and click "Sift."

Step 3: Review the Word Cloud with your students and look for trends .

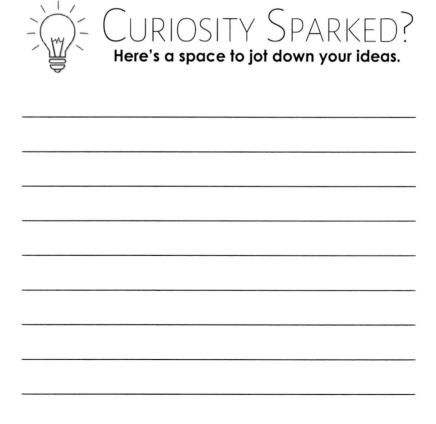

CURIOSITY SPARKED?
Here's a space to jot down your ideas.

_____

_____

_____

_____

_____

_____

_____

_____

References

Musallam, Ramsey. "Three Rules to Spark Learning." *TED: Ideas Worth Spreading*. April 2013. ted.com/talks/ramsey_musallam_3_rules_to_spark_learning.

The Spark

Allain, Rhett. "Pseudoteaching." *Wired*. February 2, 2011. wired.com/2011/02/pseudoteaching.

Rule #1: Curiosity Comes First

Lowenstein, George. "The Psychology of Curiosity: A Review and Reinterpretation." *Psychological Bulletin*, Vol. 116, 1994.

Kang, Min Jeong; Ming Hsu, Ian M. Krajbich, George Lowenstein, George; Samuel M. McClure, Joseph T. Wang, and Colin F. Camerer. "The Wick in the Candle of Learning." *Psychological Science*, December 6, 2008. int-des.com/wp-content/uploads/2013/12/PsychofCuriosity.pdf.

Gruber, Matthias J., Bernard D. Gelman, and Charan Ranganath. "States of Curiosity Modulate Hippocampus-Dependent Learning via the Dopaminergic Circuit." *Neuron*. October 2014.

Benedict, Carey. "Come On, I Thought I Knew That!" *The New York Times*, April 2011.

Kang, Min Jeong; Ming Hsu, Ian M. Krajbich, George Lowenstein, George; Samuel M. McClure, Joseph T. Wang, and Colin F. Camerer. "The Hunger for Knowledge: Neural Correlates of Curiosity." Retrieved from citeseerx.ist.psu.edu/viewdoc/download; jsessionid=37AFEB267A7818AE8E2392FBBB969367? doi=10.1.1.357.4155&rep=rep1&type=pdf.

Abrams, J.J., "The Mystery Box." *TED: Ideas Worth Spreading*. March 2007. ted.com/talks/j_j_abrams_mystery_box.

Lowenstein, George. "The Psychology of Curiosity: A Review and Reinterpretation." *Psychological Bulletin*, Vol. 116, 1994.

Spark #2: Anticipated Solution

"Hollywood Studios - Indy and the Idol - by hyku.jpg." *Wikimedia Commons*, March 8, 2009. commons.wikimedia.org/wiki/ File:Hollywood_Studios_-_Indy_and_the_idol_-_by_hyku.jpg.

Spark #3: Surprising Result

Cain, Fraser. "How Far Back Are We Looking in Time?" *Universe Today*, February 27, 2017. universetoday.com/119226/ how-far-back-are-we-looking-in-time/.

Rule #2: Embrace the Mess

Musallam, Ramsey. "Three Rules to Spark Learning." *TED: Ideas Worth Spreading*, April 2013. ted.com/talks/ ramsey_musallam_3_rules_to_spark_learning.

"John Stewart on His Daily Show Run: 'It So Far Exceeded My Expectations.'" *Fresh Air*, NPR, August 6, 2015. npr. org/2015/08/06/429851718/jon-stewart-on-his-daily-show-run-it-so-far-exceeded-my-expectations.

Mahoney, Lisa. "Contemporary Hero's Journey: The Post-Campbell Post." *Fiction Unbound*, February 20, 2015. fictionunbound.com/blog/2015/2/17/contemporary-heros-journey-the-post-campbell-post.

"BSCS 5E Instructional Model." BSCS, bscs.org/bscs-5e-instructional-model.

"Welcome to the Squishy Circuits Project Page." *Squishy Circuits*. courseweb.stthomas.edu/apthomas/SquishyCircuits/.

Conclusion

Palmer, Parker J. "The Heart of a Teacher." *Center for Courage and Renewal*. couragerenewal.org/parker/writings/heart-of-a-teacher/.

SPARK LEARNING
AT YOUR SCHOOL

BRING RAMSEY MUSALLAM TO YOUR SCHOOL OR EVENT

Ramsey Musallam offers keynotes and workshops for teachers and administrators with a focus on leveraging student curiosity for betting learning and instruction. As a full-time classroom teacher, Ramsey's insights and techniques are tangible, current and grounded in the work he does with students each day!

POPULAR PRESENTATION TOPICS INCLUDE

Sparking Curiosity—Using Questions to Fuel Instruction

Students as Heroes—The Learning Cycle as a Call to Adventure

Practical EdTech—Leveraging Simple Tools in Powerful Ways

Pseudoteaching—Diagnosis and Treatment

Engaging STEM Activities for Camps and Classrooms

Explore-Flip-Apply—An Inquiry Approach to the Flipped Classroom

CONTACT

Email: ramsey.musallam@gmail.com

Twitter: @ramusallam

Web: cyclesoflearning.com

MORE FROM
DAVE BURGESS
Consulting, Inc.

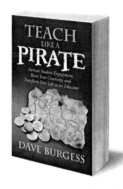

Teach Like a PIRATE
Increase Student Engagement, Boost Your Creativity, and Transform Your Life as an Educator
By Dave Burgess (@BurgessDave)

Teach Like a PIRATE is the *New York Times'* best-selling book that has sparked a worldwide educational revolution. It is part inspirational manifesto that ignites passion for the profession, and part practical road map filled with dynamic strategies to dramatically increase student engagement. Translated into multiple languages, its message resonates with educators who want to design outrageously creative lessons and transform school into a life-changing experience for students.

P is for PIRATE
Inspirational ABC's for Educators
By Dave and Shelley Burgess
(@Burgess_Shelley)

Teaching is an adventure that stretches the imagination and calls for creativity every day! In *P is for PIRATE*, husband and wife team Dave and Shelley Burgess encourage and inspire educators to make their classrooms fun and exciting places to learn. Tapping into years of personal experience and drawing on the insights of more than seventy educators, the authors offer a wealth of ideas for making learning and teaching more fulfilling than ever before.

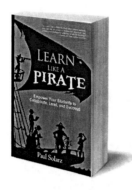

Learn Like a PIRATE

*Empower Your Students to
Collaborate, Lead, and Succeed*
By Paul Solarz (@PaulSolarz)

Today's job market demands that students be prepared to take responsibility for their lives and careers. We do them a disservice if we teach them how to earn passing grades without equipping them to take charge of their education. In *Learn Like a PIRATE*, Paul Solarz explains how to design classroom experiences that encourage students to take risks and explore their passions in a stimulating, motivating, and supportive environment where improvement, rather than grades, is the focus. Discover how student-led classrooms help students thrive and develop into self-directed, confident citizens who are capable of making smart, responsible decisions, all on their own.

Play Like a Pirate

*Engage Students with Toys, Games, and
Comics*
By Quinn Rollins (@jedikermit)

Yes! Serious learning can be seriously fun. In *Play Like a Pirate*, Quinn Rollins offers practical, engaging strategies and resources that make it easy to integrate fun into your curriculum. Regardless of the grade level you teach, you'll find inspiration and ideas that will help you engage your students in unforgettable ways.

eXPlore Like a Pirate

Gamification and Game-Inspired Course Design to Engage, Enrich, and Elevate Your Learners
By Michael Matera (@MrMatera)

Are you ready to transform your classroom into an experiential world that flourishes on collaboration and creativity? Then set sail with classroom game designer and educator Michael Matera as he reveals the possibilities and power of game-based learning. In *eXPlore Like a Pirate*, Matera serves as your experienced guide to help you apply the most motivational techniques of game play to your classroom. You'll learn gamification strategies that will work with and enhance (rather than replace) your current curriculum and discover how these engaging methods can be applied to any grade level or subject.

Lead Like a PIRATE

Make School Amazing for Your Students and Staff
By Shelley Burgess and Beth Houf
(@Burgess_Shelley, @BethHouf)

In *Lead Like a PIRATE*, education leaders Shelley Burgess and Beth Houf map out the character traits necessary to captain a school or district. You'll learn where to find the treasure that's already in your classrooms and schools—and how to bring out the very best in your educators. This book will equip and encourage you to be relentless in your quest to make school amazing for your students, staff, parents, and communities.

The Innovator's Mindset

Empower Learning, Unleash Talent, and Lead
a Culture of Creativity
By George Couros (@gcouros)

The traditional system of education requires students to hold their questions and compliantly stick to the scheduled curriculum. But our job as educators is to provide new and better opportunities for our students. It's time to recognize that compliance doesn't foster innovation, encourage critical thinking, or inspire creativity—and those are the skills our students need to succeed. In *The Innovator's Mindset*, George Couros encourages teachers and administrators to empower their learners to wonder, to explore—and to become forward-thinking leaders.

Shift This!

How to Implement Gradual Changes for
MASSIVE Impact in Your Classroom
By Joy Kirr (@JoyKirr)

Establishing a student-led culture that isn't focused on grades and homework but on individual responsibility and personalized learning, may seem like a daunting task—especially if you think you have to do it all at once. But significant change is possible, sustainable, and even easy when it happens little by little. In *Shift This!* educator and speaker Joy Kirr explains how to make gradual shifts—in your thinking, teaching, and approach to classroom design—that will have a massive impact in your classroom. Make the first shift today!

LAUNCH

Using Design Thinking to Boost Creativity and Bring Out the Maker in Every Student

By John Spencer and A.J. Juliani

(@spencerideas, @ajjuliani)

Something happens in students when they define themselves as makers and inventors and creators. They discover powerful skills—problem solving, critical thinking, and imagination—that will help them shape the world's future … our future. In *LAUNCH*, John Spencer and A.J. Juliani provide a process that can be incorporated into every class at every grade level … even if you don't consider yourself a "creative teacher." And if you dare to innovate and view creativity as an essential skill, you will empower your students to change the world—starting right now.

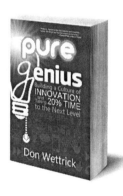

Pure Genius

Building a Culture of Innovation and Taking 20% Time to the Next Level

By Don Wettrick (@DonWettrick)

For far too long, schools have been bastions of boredom, killers of creativity, and way too comfortable with compliance and conformity. In *Pure Genius*, Don Wettrick explains how collaboration—with experts, students, and other educators—can help you create interesting, and even life-changing, opportunities for learning. Wettrick's book inspires and equips educators with a systematic blueprint for teaching innovation in any school.

Teaching Math with Google Apps

50 G Suite Activities

By Alice Keeler and Diana Herrington
(@AliceKeeler, @mathdiana)

Google Apps give teachers the opportunity to interact with students in a more meaningful way than ever before, while G Suite empowers students to be creative, critical thinkers who collaborate as they explore and learn. In *Teaching Math with Google Apps*, educators Alice Keeler and Diana Herrington demonstrate fifty different ways to bring math classes to the twenty-first century with easy-to-use technology.

Table Talk Math

A Practical Guide for Bringing Math into Everyday Conversations

By John Stevens (@Jstevens009)

Making math part of families' everyday conversations is a powerful way to help children and teens learn to love math. In *Table Talk Math*, John Stevens offers parents (and teachers!) ideas for initiating authentic, math-based conversations that will get kids to notice and be curious about all the numbers, patterns, and equations in the world around them.

The Classroom Chef

Sharpen your lessons. Season your classes. Make math meaningful.

By John Stevens and Matt Vaudrey (@Jstevens009, @MrVaudrey)

In *The Classroom Chef*, math teachers and instructional coaches John Stevens and Matt Vaudrey share their secret recipes, ingredients, and tips for serving up lessons that engage students and help them "get" math. You can use these ideas and methods as-is, or better yet, tweak them and create your own enticing educational meals. The message the authors share is that, with imagination and preparation, every teacher can be a Classroom Chef.

Instant Relevance

Using Today's Experiences in Tomorrow's Lessons

By Denis Sheeran (@MathDenisNJ)

Every day, students in schools around the world ask the question, "When am I ever going to use this in real life?" In *Instant Relevance*, author and keynote speaker Denis Sheeran equips you to create engaging lessons from experiences and events that matter to your students. Learn how to help your students see meaningful connections between the real world and what they learn in the classroom—because that's when learning sticks.

50 Things You Can Do with Google Classroom

By Alice Keeler and Libbi Miller
(@alicekeeler, @MillerLibbi)

It can be challenging to add new technology to the classroom, but it's a must if students are going to be well-equipped for the future. Alice Keeler and Libbi Miller shorten the learning curve by providing a thorough overview of the Google Classroom App. Part of Google Apps for Education (GAfE), Google Classroom was specifically designed to help teachers save time by streamlining the process of going digital. Complete with screenshots, *50 Things You Can Do with Google Classroom* provides ideas and step-by-step instructions to help teachers implement this powerful tool.

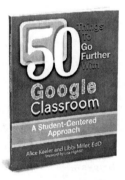

50 Things to Go Further with Google Classroom

A Student-Centered Approach

By Alice Keeler and Libbi Miller
(@alicekeeler, @MillerLibbi)

Today's technology empowers educators to move away from the traditional classroom where teachers lead and students work independently—each doing the same thing. In *50 Things to Go Further with Google Classroom: A Student-Centered Approach*, authors and educators Alice Keeler and Libbi Miller offer inspiration and resources to help you create a digitally rich, engaging, student-centered environment. They show you how to tap into the power of individualized learning that is possible with Google Classroom.

140 Twitter Tips for Educators

Get Connected, Grow Your Professional Learning Network, and Reinvigorate Your Career

By Brad Currie, Billy Krakower, and Scott Rocco (@bradmcurrie, @wkrakower, @ScottRRocco)

Whatever questions you have about education or about how you can be even better at your job, you'll find ideas, resources, and a vibrant network of professionals ready to help you on Twitter. In *140 Twitter Tips for Educators*, #Satchat hosts and founders of Evolving Educators, Brad Currie, Billy Krakower, and Scott Rocco, offer step-by-step instructions to help you master the basics of Twitter, build an online following, and become a Twitter rock star.

Ditch That Textbook

Free Your Teaching and Revolutionize Your Classroom

By Matt Miller (@jmattmiller)

Textbooks are symbols of centuries of old education. They're often outdated as soon as they hit students' desks. Acting "by the textbook" implies compliance and a lack of creativity. It's time to ditch those textbooks—and those textbook assumptions about learning!

In *Ditch That Textbook*, teacher and blogger Matt Miller encourages educators to throw out meaningless, pedestrian teaching and learning practices. He empowers them to evolve and improve on old, standard teaching methods. *Ditch That Textbook* is a support system, toolbox, and manifesto to help educators free their teaching and revolutionize their classrooms.

Your School Rocks ... So Tell People!

Passionately Pitch and Promote the Positives
Happening on Your Campus
By Ryan McLane and Eric Lowe
(@McLane_Ryan, @EricLowe21)

Great things are happening in your school every day. The problem is, no one beyond your school walls knows about them. School principals Ryan McLane and Eric Lowe want to help you get the word out! In *Your School Rocks ... So Tell People!* McLane and Lowe offer more than seventy immediately actionable tips along with easy-to-follow instructions and links to video tutorials. This practical guide will equip you to create an effective and manageable communication strategy using social-media tools. Learn how to keep your students' families and community connected, informed, and excited about what's going on in your school.

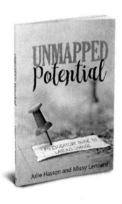

Unmapped Potential

An Educator's Guide to Lasting Change
By Julie Hasson and Missy Lennard
(@PPrincipals)

No matter where you are in your educational career, chances are you have, at times, felt overwhelmed and overworked. Maybe you feel that way right now. If so, you aren't alone. But the more important news is that things can get better! You simply need the right map to guide you from frustrated to fulfilled. *Unmapped Potential* offers advice and practical strategies to help you find your unique path to becoming the kind of educator—the kind of person—you want to be.

The Zen Teacher

Creating FOCUS, SIMPLICITY, and TRANQUILITY in the Classroom

By Dan Tricarico (@thezenteacher)

Teachers have incredible power to influence, even improve, the future. In *The Zen Teacher*, educator, blogger, and speaker Dan Tricarico provides practical, easy-to-use techniques to help teachers be their best—unrushed and fully focused—so they can maximize their performance and improve their quality of life. In this introductory guide, Dan Tricarico explains what it means to develop a Zen practice—something that has nothing to do with religion and everything to do with your ability to thrive in the classroom.

How Much Water Do We Have?

5 Success Principles for Conquering Any Change and Thriving in Times of Change

By Pete Nunweiler with Kris Nunweiler

In *How Much Water Do We Have?* Pete Nunweiler identifies five key elements that are necessary for the success of any goal, life transition, or challenge: information, planning, motivation, support, and leadership. Referring to these elements as the 5 Waters of Success, Pete explains that, like the water we drink, you need them to thrive in today's rapidly paced world. If you're feeling stressed out, overwhelmed, or uncertain at work or at home, pause and look for the signs of dehydration. Learn how to find, acquire, and use the 5 Waters of Success—so you can share them with your team and family members.

The Writing on the Classroom Wall

How Posting Your Most Passionate Beliefs about Education Can Empower Your Students, Propel Your Growth, and Lead to a Lifetime of Learning

By Steve Wyborney (@SteveWyborney)

In *The Writing on the Classroom Wall*, Steve Wyborney explains how posting and discussing Big Ideas can lead to deeper learning. You'll learn why sharing your ideas will sharpen and refine them. You'll also be encouraged to know that the Big Ideas you share don't have to be profound to make a profound impact on learning. In fact, Steve explains, it's okay if some of your ideas fall off the wall. What matters most is sharing them.

Kids Deserve It!

Pushing Boundaries and Challenging Conventional Thinking

By Todd Nesloney and Adam Welcome (@TechNinjaTodd, @awelcome)

In *Kids Deserve It!*, Todd and Adam encourage you to think big and make learning fun and meaningful for students. Their high-tech, high-touch, and highly engaging practices will inspire you to take risks, shake up the status quo, and be a champion for your students. While you're at it, you just might rediscover why you became an educator in the first place.

Escaping the School Leader's Dunk Tank

How to Prevail When Others Want to See You Drown

By Rebecca Coda and Rick Jetter

(@RebeccaCoda, @RickJetter)

No school leader is immune to the effects of discrimination, bad politics, revenge, or ego-driven coworkers. These kinds of dunk-tank situations can make an educator's life miserable. By sharing real-life stories and insightful research, the authors (who are dunk-tank survivors themselves) equip school leaders with the practical knowledge and emotional tools necessary to survive and, better yet, avoid getting "dunked."

Start. Right. Now.

Teach and Lead for Excellence

By Todd Whitaker, Jeff Zoul, and Jimmy Casas

(@ToddWhitaker, @Jeff_Zoul, @casas_jimmy)

In their work leading up to *Start. Right. Now.* Todd Whitaker, Jeff Zoul, and Jimmy Casas studied educators from across the nation and discovered four key behaviors of excellence: Excellent leaders and teachers Know the Way, Show the Way, Go the Way, and Grow Each Day. If you are ready to take the first step toward excellence, this motivating book will put you on the right path.

Master the Media
How Teaching Media Literacy Can Save Our Plugged-in World
By Julie Smith

Written to help teachers and parents educate the next generation, *Master the Media* explains the history, purpose, and messages behind the media. The point isn't to get kids to unplug; it's to help them make informed choices, understand the difference between truth and lies, and discern perception from reality. Critical thinking leads to smarter decisions—and it's why media literacy can save the world.